Lysa Wren

Breaking Down Gender Norms in Velmar – Unfiltered

Abdul Koroma

ISBN: 9781779697936
Imprint: Telephasic Workshop
Copyright © 2024 Abdul Koroma.
All Rights Reserved.

Contents

Introduction

The Unconventional Activist

Lysa Wren's Early Years

Lysa Wren was born in the vibrant town of Velmar, a place where tradition and modernity collided in a colorful tapestry of culture and expectation. From a young age, Lysa exhibited a keen awareness of the world around her, often questioning the rigid gender norms that dictated the lives of those in her community. Her early years were marked by a sense of curiosity and a yearning for authenticity that would later shape her identity as an activist.

Growing up in a household that valued education and creativity, Lysa found solace in books and art. She often spent hours immersed in literature, drawn to stories that challenged societal norms. One of her early influences was the works of Virginia Woolf, whose exploration of gender fluidity resonated deeply with Lysa. Woolf's concept of the "androgynous mind" became a cornerstone of Lysa's developing philosophy, inspiring her to envision a world where individuals could transcend binary classifications.

However, Lysa's journey was not without its challenges. As a child, she faced the harsh realities of bullying and ostracism for her non-conforming behavior. The societal pressures to fit into predefined gender roles were suffocating. Lysa often found herself at odds with her peers, who struggled to understand her unique perspective. This isolation led to moments of profound self-doubt, as Lysa grappled with her identity in a world that seemed determined to impose limitations on her existence.

In her formative years, Lysa began to articulate her feelings through writing. Poetry became her refuge, a means to express the turmoil she felt inside. Lines such as:

"The world insists I wear a mask, But I am more than what they ask."

reflected her internal struggle and desire for authenticity. This creative outlet not only provided an escape but also laid the groundwork for her future activism. Through her words, Lysa began to forge connections with others who felt similarly marginalized, creating a small but supportive community of like-minded individuals.

Lysa's family played a pivotal role in her early development. Her parents, while initially struggling to understand her unconventional nature, eventually became her strongest allies. They encouraged her to embrace her identity and fostered an environment where open dialogue was valued. This support was crucial in helping Lysa navigate the complexities of her emerging identity, allowing her to explore the nuances of gender and sexuality without fear of judgment.

As Lysa entered her teenage years, she became increasingly aware of the broader societal issues surrounding LGBTQ rights. The visibility of LGBTQ activists in media and politics inspired her to engage more actively in discussions about gender and sexuality. She began attending local meetings and events, where she met individuals who shared her passion for change. These experiences were transformative, igniting a fire within her to challenge the status quo.

The importance of representation in media also became a significant theme in Lysa's early years. She recognized that the stories told in the mainstream often excluded or misrepresented those who did not conform to traditional gender norms. This realization fueled her desire to create her narrative, one that celebrated diversity and authenticity. Lysa's early encounters with activism were marked by a strong commitment to amplifying marginalized voices and advocating for inclusive representation.

In summary, Lysa Wren's early years were characterized by a profound exploration of identity, creativity, and resilience. Her experiences of isolation, coupled with the support of her family and the influence of literature, laid the foundation for her future activism. As she navigated the complexities of gender norms in Velmar, Lysa emerged as a fearless advocate for authenticity and self-expression, setting the stage for the impactful journey that lay ahead.

Discovering Her Identity

Lysa Wren's journey toward self-discovery was not merely a personal endeavor; it was a profound exploration of the intricate tapestry of identity, culture, and societal expectations. Growing up in Velmar, a community steeped in traditional gender norms, Lysa faced the daunting task of navigating her own identity amidst the rigid frameworks imposed by society.

The Struggle with Conformity

As a child, Lysa exhibited interests and behaviors that diverged from the conventional expectations of her gender. Engaging in activities typically associated with masculinity, such as sports and adventurous play, she often found herself at odds with her peers and the adults around her. This dissonance can be understood through the lens of Judith Butler's theory of gender performativity, which posits that gender is not an innate quality but rather a series of acts and performances dictated by societal norms. Lysa's early experiences exemplified this theory, as she grappled with the pressure to conform to the gender roles expected of her.

$$G = P_1 + P_2 + ... + P_n \qquad (1)$$

Where G represents gender identity, and P_i represents the various performances that contribute to the construction of that identity. For Lysa, the performances expected of her did not resonate with her true self, leading to a profound internal conflict.

The Role of Reflection

The turning point in Lysa's journey came during her teenage years when she began to engage in introspective practices. Journaling became a sanctuary for her thoughts, allowing her to articulate feelings that had long been suppressed. This reflective practice not only served as a therapeutic outlet but also facilitated a deeper understanding of her identity. Research indicates that self-reflection can significantly enhance one's self-concept and emotional well-being, a phenomenon that Lysa experienced firsthand.

Finding Community

As Lysa ventured into the world of LGBTQ activism, she discovered a supportive community that embraced her for who she was. This newfound sense of belonging was crucial in affirming her identity. The importance of community in the identity formation process is well-documented in social identity theory, which posits that individuals derive a sense of self from their group affiliations. Lysa's involvement in LGBTQ groups provided her with the validation and encouragement needed to embrace her identity fully.

The Impact of Representation

Representation played a pivotal role in Lysa's self-discovery. Exposure to diverse narratives through literature, film, and social media allowed her to see reflections of herself in the stories of others. Figures like RuPaul and Ellen DeGeneres, who openly challenged gender norms and celebrated their identities, inspired Lysa to reclaim her narrative. The representation theory posits that seeing oneself in media can lead to increased self-acceptance and empowerment, which was evident in Lysa's journey.

Navigating Intersectionality

Lysa's identity was further complicated by the intersectionality of her experiences. As a queer individual in a society that often marginalized multiple identities, she faced unique challenges. Kimberlé Crenshaw's theory of intersectionality highlights how overlapping social identities can create distinct modes of discrimination and privilege. Lysa's understanding of her identity was thus shaped not only by her gender and sexual orientation but also by her cultural background and socio-economic status.

Embracing Authenticity

Ultimately, the culmination of Lysa's journey toward self-discovery was the embrace of her authenticity. She learned that true liberation comes from accepting oneself wholly, flaws and all. This realization echoes the sentiments of bell hooks, who emphasized the importance of self-love and authenticity in the pursuit of personal and collective liberation. Lysa's journey became a testament to the power of embracing one's identity in a world that often seeks to impose conformity.

In conclusion, Lysa Wren's discovery of her identity was a multifaceted process influenced by societal expectations, community support, representation, and intersectionality. Her journey serves as an inspiring reminder that the path to self-acceptance is often fraught with challenges, yet it is also filled with the potential for profound personal growth and empowerment.

Navigating Gender Norms in Velmar

In the vibrant yet complex society of Velmar, gender norms have long dictated the parameters of identity, behavior, and social acceptance. Lysa Wren, through her unique lens as an unconventional activist, embarked on a journey to navigate and dismantle these entrenched norms, revealing both the struggles and triumphs that accompany such a quest.

Understanding Gender Norms

Gender norms are societal expectations that dictate how individuals should behave based on their perceived gender. These norms can be deeply rooted in cultural, historical, and social contexts, often leading to rigid binaries that fail to encompass the full spectrum of human experience. In Velmar, traditional gender roles have been reinforced through various institutions, including education, religion, and media.

For instance, boys were often encouraged to embody traits associated with masculinity—strength, stoicism, and dominance—while girls were socialized to embrace femininity characterized by nurturing, passivity, and appearance. These constructs not only limit personal expression but also perpetuate discrimination against those who dare to defy them.

Theoretical Framework

To understand Lysa Wren's approach to navigating these norms, we can draw upon Judith Butler's theory of gender performativity. Butler posits that gender is not an innate quality but rather a series of performances shaped by societal expectations. This perspective allows for a critical examination of how individuals, including Lysa, can subvert traditional norms by altering their performances.

$$G = P_1 + P_2 + P_3 + \ldots + P_n \tag{2}$$

Where G represents gender, and P_i denotes the various performances that contribute to the construction of gender identity. Lysa's journey exemplifies this equation; by embracing fluidity and challenging binary constructs, she redefined her own identity and influenced others in Velmar to do the same.

Challenges Faced

Navigating gender norms in Velmar was not without its challenges. Lysa encountered significant backlash from traditionalists who viewed her activism as a threat to societal stability. For example, during a local community meeting aimed at discussing LGBTQ rights, Lysa was met with hostility from attendees who believed that her ideas would undermine family values.

Additionally, Lysa faced internal struggles, grappling with the fear of rejection and ostracization from her peers. The tension between her authentic self and societal expectations created a battleground within her, leading to episodes of self-doubt and questioning.

Strategies for Change

Despite these challenges, Lysa employed several strategies to navigate and ultimately reshape the gender landscape in Velmar:

- **Education and Awareness:** Lysa organized workshops and discussions that focused on gender diversity, aiming to educate the public about non-binary identities and the importance of inclusive language.

- **Community Building:** By forming alliances with local LGBTQ organizations, Lysa fostered a sense of community among those who felt marginalized, providing them with a safe space to express their identities.

- **Artistic Expression:** Lysa utilized art as a medium for activism, creating visual and performance art that challenged traditional gender roles and celebrated fluidity. Her installations often sparked conversations and encouraged viewers to reflect on their own beliefs.

Impact on Velmar Society

Lysa Wren's efforts began to yield tangible results. Her activism inspired a new generation of individuals in Velmar to embrace their identities unapologetically. As more people shared their stories, the community witnessed a gradual shift in attitudes towards gender norms.

For example, a local high school implemented an inclusive curriculum that addressed gender diversity, allowing students to explore their identities within a supportive environment. Furthermore, the annual Velmar Pride event, initially met with resistance, transformed into a vibrant celebration of diversity, drawing participation from all corners of the community.

Conclusion

Navigating gender norms in Velmar was a multifaceted endeavor that required courage, resilience, and an unwavering commitment to authenticity. Lysa Wren's journey exemplifies the power of challenging societal constructs and the importance of fostering an inclusive environment where all individuals can thrive.

As Velmar continues to evolve, Lysa's impact serves as a reminder that breaking down gender norms is not just a personal journey but a collective movement towards a more equitable society.

A Unique Perspective on LGBTQ Activism

Lysa Wren's approach to LGBTQ activism is characterized by an unyielding commitment to authenticity and inclusivity, which sets her apart from many traditional activists. Her unique perspective is shaped by her personal experiences, cultural background, and a deep understanding of intersectionality, making her activism not only relevant but also necessary in today's society.

Intersectionality and Its Importance

At the core of Lysa's activism is the concept of **intersectionality**, a term coined by legal scholar Kimberlé Crenshaw in 1989. This framework emphasizes how various social identities—such as race, gender, sexuality, and class—interact to create overlapping systems of discrimination or disadvantage. Lysa recognizes that LGBTQ individuals are not a monolith; their experiences are influenced by their other identities. For instance, a Black transgender woman may face different challenges than a white cisgender gay man.

Lysa often cites the equation:

$$D = f(I_1, I_2, ..., I_n) \tag{3}$$

where D represents discrimination, and $I_1, I_2, ..., I_n$ are the various intersecting identities. This equation encapsulates her belief that understanding the complexity of identity is crucial for effective activism.

Challenging Mainstream Narratives

Lysa's activism challenges mainstream narratives within the LGBTQ community that often prioritize certain identities over others. For example, she critiques the tendency of some movements to focus predominantly on issues affecting white, cisgender, gay men while neglecting the voices and struggles of LGBTQ people of color, transgender individuals, and non-binary folks. By amplifying these marginalized voices, Lysa aims to create a more inclusive dialogue that reflects the diversity of the community.

The Role of Art and Expression

Another unique aspect of Lysa's activism is her emphasis on the role of art and self-expression as powerful tools for change. She often collaborates with local artists and writers to create platforms that showcase diverse narratives within the LGBTQ community. Lysa believes that art can transcend barriers and foster empathy, making it an essential component of her activism.

Her literary influences, including Audre Lorde and James Baldwin, have inspired her to use storytelling as a means to challenge stereotypes and promote understanding. Lysa often states, *"Art is not just a reflection of society; it is a catalyst for transformation."* This perspective underscores her belief that activism should not only be about policy change but also about reshaping cultural narratives.

Engagement with Technology

In the digital age, Lysa has harnessed the power of social media to amplify her message and engage with a wider audience. She recognizes that technology can be a double-edged sword—while it offers a platform for marginalized voices, it also exposes activists to backlash and harassment. Lysa navigates this landscape with a strategic approach, using her online presence to foster dialogue and build community.

Her initiative, the **"Proud & Unapologetic"** campaign, exemplifies this engagement. Through a series of online workshops and discussions, Lysa encourages participants to share their stories and experiences, creating a sense of solidarity and support. This initiative has not only empowered individuals but has also sparked broader conversations about the complexities of identity and activism.

Confronting Backlash and Criticism

Lysa is no stranger to backlash. Her outspoken nature and willingness to challenge the status quo have led to criticism from various quarters, including those within the LGBTQ community. However, she views criticism as an opportunity for growth and dialogue. In her words, *"Every challenge is a chance to educate and evolve."*

She often employs the following strategies to confront criticism:

+ **Listening and Learning:** Lysa believes in the importance of listening to opposing viewpoints, as this can lead to a deeper understanding of the issues at hand.

- **Engaging in Dialogue:** Rather than dismissing critics, she invites them into conversations, fostering an environment where constructive discourse can occur.

- **Staying True to Her Values:** Lysa remains steadfast in her commitment to authenticity, ensuring that her activism aligns with her core beliefs and values.

Conclusion

Lysa Wren's unique perspective on LGBTQ activism is a testament to the power of authenticity, inclusivity, and intersectionality. Her approach challenges traditional narratives, embraces the arts, leverages technology, and confronts criticism head-on. By doing so, she not only paves the way for her own activism but also inspires others to engage in the ongoing struggle for equality and justice. As Lysa often reminds her followers, *"Our stories are our strength; let's share them unapologetically."*

Challenging the Status Quo

In the vibrant tapestry of LGBTQ activism, challenging the status quo serves as a crucial thread that binds together the narratives of countless individuals. For Lysa Wren, this challenge was not merely a personal endeavor; it was a clarion call for societal transformation in Velmar. The status quo, often characterized by rigid gender norms and binary classifications, perpetuates a system that marginalizes those who dare to defy conventional expectations. Lysa's journey into activism was fueled by an acute awareness of these societal constraints and a determination to dismantle them.

Theoretical frameworks such as Judith Butler's concept of gender performativity provide a foundation for understanding the nuances of Lysa's activism. Butler posits that gender is not an innate quality but rather a series of performances that individuals enact based on societal expectations. This perspective invites us to question the very fabric of our identities and the roles we are assigned. Lysa's challenge to the status quo involved exposing the performative nature of gender and advocating for a more fluid understanding of identity. She often cited Butler's work in her speeches, emphasizing that true liberation comes from recognizing the constructed nature of gender roles.

One of the primary problems Lysa identified in Velmar was the pervasive influence of binary constructs that dictated how individuals should express their gender. In her early activism, she encountered resistance from traditionalists who viewed her ideas as a threat to societal cohesion. This conflict highlighted the deep-seated fears surrounding the disruption of established norms. Lysa's response was to engage in dialogues that illuminated the limitations of binary thinking, using examples from her own life to demonstrate the fluidity of identity. She often recounted her experiences of feeling confined by societal expectations, illustrating how these norms stifled authenticity and self-expression.

Lysa's activism was not confined to theoretical discussions; she took to the streets, organizing workshops and community forums aimed at educating others about gender diversity.   One notable event was the "Gender Spectrum Symposium," where speakers from various backgrounds shared their experiences of navigating gender norms. This symposium became a pivotal moment in Velmar, drawing attention to the diversity of gender identities and encouraging attendees to embrace their authentic selves. The event was met with both enthusiasm and backlash, revealing the polarized views on gender in the community.

An essential aspect of challenging the status quo involves the use of inclusive language. Lysa advocated for a shift in the language used to describe gender, emphasizing the importance of pronouns and terms that reflect individuals' identities. She often quoted the phrase, "Language shapes reality," to underscore how the words we choose can either empower or diminish marginalized voices. By promoting the use of non-binary pronouns and inclusive terminology, Lysa sought to create a more welcoming environment for those who had long been silenced.

Moreover, Lysa's activism was deeply intertwined with the concept of intersectionality, a term coined by Kimberlé Crenshaw.   Intersectionality recognizes that individuals experience overlapping identities that influence their experiences of oppression and privilege. Lysa's approach to challenging the status quo was not only about gender but also about addressing the intersections of race, class, and sexual orientation. She understood that the fight for LGBTQ rights could not be separated from broader social justice movements. By highlighting these intersections, Lysa was able to forge alliances with other activist groups, expanding the reach and impact of her message.

In her writings, Lysa often reflected on the importance of empathy in challenging societal norms. She believed that fostering understanding among diverse groups was essential for dismantling prejudice. One poignant example she shared was her interaction with a group of conservative activists who initially opposed her views. Through patient dialogue and shared personal stories, Lysa was able to bridge the gap between differing perspectives, illustrating that empathy could pave the way for meaningful change.

Ultimately, Lysa Wren's commitment to challenging the status quo was a testament to her belief in the power of individual stories. She understood that every act of defiance against societal norms contributed to a larger narrative of resistance and resilience. By sharing her journey and uplifting the voices of others,

Lysa not only challenged the status quo but also inspired a new generation of activists to continue the fight for authenticity and acceptance. Her legacy serves as a reminder that the journey toward equality is ongoing, and that each of us has a role to play in dismantling the barriers that divide us.

In conclusion, Lysa Wren's approach to challenging the status quo in Velmar was multifaceted, incorporating theoretical insights, personal narratives, and community engagement. Her work exemplifies the essential nature of activism in the face of entrenched norms, highlighting the need for continued dialogue, education, and empathy in the pursuit of a more inclusive society. As we reflect on her contributions, we are reminded that the path to change is often fraught with challenges, but it is also paved with the courage and determination of those who dare to question the world around them.

The Journey Begins

The journey of Lysa Wren into the world of activism was not merely a step, but rather a leap into the unknown, one that would challenge her deeply ingrained perceptions of gender and identity. It began in the heart of Velmar, a town where tradition clashed with the burgeoning acceptance of diversity. As she stepped into her role as an activist, Lysa found herself at the intersection of personal growth and social change.

At the core of her journey was the realization that activism is as much about personal transformation as it is about societal change. This concept resonates with the theory of *intersectionality*, introduced by Kimberlé Crenshaw, which posits that various social identities (such as race, gender, and sexual orientation) intersect to create unique modes of discrimination and privilege. Lysa's own identity as a queer individual navigating the rigid gender norms of Velmar propelled her to seek understanding and solidarity within her community.

$$\text{Activism} = f(\text{Identity, Community, Change}) \qquad (4)$$

In this equation, f represents the function of activism, driven by the variables of identity, community, and change. Lysa's identity as a non-binary individual became the catalyst for her activism. She recognized that her experiences were not isolated; they were part of a larger narrative that required a collective voice to enact change.

Lysa's first significant act of activism came during a local pride event, where she took the stage to speak about the importance of embracing one's identity. Her words were a blend of vulnerability and strength, echoing the struggles of many who felt marginalized. She articulated the challenges faced by those who defy conventional gender norms, using her own story as a powerful example. This moment marked the beginning of her commitment to advocating for inclusivity and acceptance.

However, the journey was not without its challenges. Lysa faced backlash from conservative factions within Velmar, who viewed her activism as a threat to their traditional values. This opposition, while disheartening, only fueled her resolve. She understood that the path to change is often paved with resistance, and she embraced this reality as part of her journey.

The importance of community support became evident as Lysa began to connect with other activists. Through workshops, discussions, and online platforms, she discovered a network of individuals who shared her passion for change. This sense of belonging was crucial; it provided her with the strength to continue her work even in the face of adversity. Lysa often cited the work of Audre Lorde, who famously stated, "I am not free while any woman is unfree, even when her shackles are very different from my own." This sentiment resonated deeply with Lysa, reinforcing her belief in the power of collective action.

As Lysa's visibility grew, so did her platform. She began to utilize social media as a means of reaching a broader audience, sharing her experiences and insights while amplifying the voices of others. The digital landscape became a space for dialogue, where stories of struggle and triumph could be shared and celebrated. Her initiative, the "Proud & Unapologetic" movement, emerged as a response to the need for a more inclusive narrative around gender and sexuality.

This movement was not merely a campaign; it was a call to action for individuals to embrace their identities unapologetically. Lysa organized events that encouraged self-expression, fostering a safe space for individuals to explore their identities without fear of judgment. The impact of these gatherings was profound, as participants found solace in shared experiences and cultivated a sense of community.

Yet, with increased visibility came scrutiny. Lysa faced criticism from both within and outside the LGBTQ community. Some questioned her authenticity, while others dismissed her activism as a phase. In response, she leaned into the discomfort, using it as an opportunity to educate and engage in meaningful conversations. Lysa's resilience became a hallmark of her activism, embodying the idea that vulnerability is a strength, not a weakness.

As she navigated these challenges, Lysa remained committed to her mission. She understood that the journey was ongoing, marked by both victories and setbacks. The importance of self-care and mental health became paramount, as she sought to maintain her well-being amidst the demands of activism. Lysa often reminded herself of the words of Maya Angelou: "You may encounter many defeats, but you must not be defeated."

In conclusion, the journey of Lysa Wren was one of self-discovery, resilience, and unwavering commitment to change. It was a journey that began with a single step but evolved into a movement that challenged the very fabric of gender norms in Velmar. Through her experiences, Lysa not only broke down barriers but also inspired others to embrace their identities and advocate for a more inclusive society. The journey was just beginning, and Lysa Wren was determined to lead the way.

Finding Support and Allies

In the tumultuous landscape of LGBTQ activism, finding support and allies is not merely beneficial; it is essential for survival and success. Lysa Wren's journey in Velmar exemplifies the importance of cultivating a network of allies who share the vision of dismantling oppressive gender norms and advocating for equal rights. This section delves into the dynamics of allyship, the challenges faced in establishing these connections, and the transformative impact of solidarity in the pursuit of social justice.

The Importance of Allyship

Allyship can be defined as the active support of marginalized groups by individuals who do not identify as part of those groups. In the context of LGBTQ activism, allies play a crucial role in amplifying voices, challenging discrimination, and fostering inclusive environments. Lysa understood that her fight was not solely hers; it was a collective struggle that required the involvement of diverse stakeholders. Theories of allyship, such as those proposed by [?], emphasize the necessity for allies to educate themselves, listen to the experiences of marginalized individuals, and use their privilege to advocate for change.

Building a Network

Finding allies in Velmar was not without its challenges. Lysa faced initial resistance from those who adhered to traditional gender roles and conservative values. However, through persistent outreach and engagement, she began to build a network of supporters. This included fellow activists, community organizations, and even sympathetic individuals within local government. Lysa organized workshops and discussion panels, inviting allies to learn about LGBTQ issues and the importance of intersectionality, as highlighted by [?].

$$\text{Allyship} = \text{Education} + \text{Empathy} + \text{Action} \qquad (5)$$

This equation illustrates that true allyship requires a combination of understanding the issues at hand, empathizing with the struggles faced by marginalized groups, and taking concrete actions to support those groups.

Challenges in Finding Allies

Despite her efforts, Lysa encountered significant obstacles in her quest for allies. Many individuals were hesitant to engage due to fear of backlash or social ostracism. The phenomenon of *bystander apathy*, as described by [?], often left potential allies paralyzed in the face of injustice. Lysa recognized that addressing these fears was crucial. She initiated dialogues that emphasized the importance of standing up against discrimination, even when it was uncomfortable.

The Role of Community Organizations

Community organizations served as vital support systems for Lysa and her allies. Groups such as the Velmar LGBTQ Coalition provided resources, training, and a platform for collective action. Lysa collaborated with these organizations to host events that not only educated the public but also showcased the stories of LGBTQ individuals. This approach fostered a sense of belonging and encouraged more people to step forward as allies.

Real-Life Examples of Allyship

One of the most impactful moments in Lysa's journey came during a local pride event, where she was joined by a diverse group of allies, including parents of LGBTQ youth, educators, and local business owners. This gathering symbolized the power of solidarity and the collective strength of community. Lysa recalls the moment when a local business owner, previously silent on LGBTQ issues, publicly declared support for marriage equality. This act of bravery inspired others to follow suit, demonstrating the ripple effect of allyship.

The Transformative Impact of Solidarity

The support Lysa garnered from allies not only bolstered her activism but also transformed the cultural landscape of Velmar. As more individuals began to advocate for LGBTQ rights, the community witnessed a shift in attitudes. The theory of *social contagion* posits that behaviors and attitudes can spread through social networks, leading to widespread change [?]. Lysa's experience illustrated this phenomenon as her allies inspired their friends and family to engage in conversations about gender norms and LGBTQ rights.

Conclusion

In conclusion, finding support and allies was a pivotal aspect of Lysa Wren's activism in Velmar. Through education, community engagement, and the cultivation of allyship, she was able to create a powerful network that challenged the status quo and advocated for change. The journey toward equality is not one that can be undertaken alone; it requires the collective efforts of individuals from all walks of life. As Lysa Wren's story illustrates, the fight for LGBTQ rights is strengthened by the unwavering support of allies who are willing to stand up, speak out, and take action.

Lysa Wren's Impact on Velmar Society

Lysa Wren's emergence as a pivotal figure in LGBTQ activism has left an indelible mark on the society of Velmar, a town that has historically grappled with rigid gender norms and traditional values. Her journey serves as a case study in the transformative power of individual activism, illustrating how one person's voice can catalyze societal change.

Theoretical Framework

To understand Lysa Wren's impact, we can apply the *Social Change Theory*, which posits that individuals can influence societal structures through collective action and advocacy. This theory emphasizes the role of grassroots movements in challenging entrenched norms and fostering inclusivity. Lysa's activism aligns with the principles of this theory, as she mobilized community members to confront and dismantle systemic barriers faced by the LGBTQ population in Velmar.

Challenging Gender Norms

Lysa's efforts have been instrumental in challenging the binary constructs of gender that have dominated Velmar's cultural landscape. By advocating for the acceptance of non-binary identities, she has fostered a dialogue that encourages individuals to embrace their authentic selves. This shift is exemplified by the increased visibility of non-binary individuals in local media and public forums, challenging the traditional male-female dichotomy.

$$\text{Visibility} = f(\text{Advocacy, Community Engagement, Media Representation}) \quad (6)$$

This equation suggests that visibility in society is a function of active advocacy, community engagement, and representation in media. Lysa's initiatives have led to a notable increase in representation, as evidenced by the inclusion of non-binary characters in local theater productions and literature.

Creating Safe Spaces

One of Lysa's most significant contributions has been the establishment of safe spaces for LGBTQ individuals in Velmar. These spaces serve as havens where individuals can express their identities without fear of discrimination or violence. The creation of support groups and community centers has provided essential resources for mental health, education, and social support.

$$\text{Safe Space Impact} = \frac{\text{Number of Participants}}{\text{Incidents of Discrimination}} \quad (7)$$

This equation illustrates that as the number of participants in safe spaces increases, there tends to be a decrease in reported incidents of discrimination, indicating the protective effect of these environments.

Educational Initiatives

Lysa's impact extends to educational initiatives aimed at fostering understanding and acceptance among the youth of Velmar. She has spearheaded workshops in local schools that address topics such as gender identity, sexual orientation, and the importance of empathy. These educational programs have been pivotal in reshaping the perspectives of young individuals, promoting a culture of inclusivity.

Community Engagement and Activism

The *Proud & Unapologetic* movement, founded by Lysa, has galvanized community engagement through rallies, art exhibitions, and public discussions. These events have not only raised awareness about LGBTQ issues but have also encouraged participation from allies and marginalized groups alike. The movement's slogan, "Our Voices, Our Stories," encapsulates the essence of collective empowerment.

Legislative Advocacy

Lysa's activism has also had a profound impact on local legislation. Through persistent advocacy, she has influenced policymakers to consider the inclusion of LGBTQ rights in local laws. Her efforts played a crucial role in the passing of the *Velmar Equality Act*, which provides protections against discrimination in employment, housing, and public accommodations for LGBTQ individuals.

$$\text{Legislative Change} = \text{Advocacy Efforts} \times \text{Public Support} \tag{8}$$

This equation emphasizes that legislative change is a product of sustained advocacy efforts multiplied by the level of public support, which Lysa has effectively cultivated through her outreach and education.

Cultural Shifts

The cultural landscape of Velmar has shifted significantly due to Lysa's influence. Events such as the annual *Velmar Pride Festival* have become platforms for celebration and visibility, showcasing the diversity of identities within the LGBTQ community. These cultural shifts have fostered a more accepting and inclusive environment, encouraging individuals to live authentically.

Conclusion

In conclusion, Lysa Wren's impact on Velmar society is profound and multifaceted. Through her advocacy, she has not only challenged and reshaped gender norms but has also created safe spaces, fostered educational initiatives, and influenced legislative changes. Her journey exemplifies the power of activism in transforming societal attitudes, making Velmar a more inclusive place for all its residents. As Lysa continues her work, her legacy will undoubtedly inspire future generations to embrace authenticity and advocate for equality.

The Importance of Authenticity

In the realm of LGBTQ activism, authenticity serves as the cornerstone of effective advocacy and individual empowerment. Lysa Wren's journey underscores the profound impact that embracing one's true self can have, not only on personal growth but also on societal change. Authenticity, in this context, can be defined as the alignment of one's self-perception with their outward expression, leading to a genuine representation of identity.

Theoretical Framework

The concept of authenticity is deeply rooted in existential philosophy, particularly in the works of thinkers like Jean-Paul Sartre and Simone de Beauvoir. Sartre posited that existence precedes essence, suggesting that individuals must create their own identity through choices and actions. This framework resonates strongly within LGBTQ communities, where societal norms often impose restrictive identities. Authenticity becomes a radical act of self-definition, allowing individuals to reject imposed labels and embrace their multifaceted selves.

Moreover, psychological theories, such as Carl Rogers' Humanistic Psychology, emphasize the importance of congruence between self-image and experience. Rogers argued that individuals who are authentic experience greater psychological well-being. This notion is particularly relevant for LGBTQ individuals, who often face pressure to conform to societal expectations that conflict with their true identities. By fostering authenticity, activists like Lysa Wren not only advocate for personal liberation but also challenge the systemic barriers that perpetuate discrimination.

Challenges to Authenticity

Despite its importance, authenticity is frequently challenged by various societal factors. Internalized homophobia, societal stigma, and fear of rejection can create significant barriers to self-acceptance. Lysa Wren's own experiences reflect these struggles; she navigated a landscape filled with conflicting messages about gender and sexuality. The pressure to conform to binary norms often leads individuals to suppress their true selves, resulting in mental health issues such as anxiety and depression.

Additionally, the concept of "performative activism" has emerged as a critique of superficial expressions of support for LGBTQ rights. Many individuals and organizations engage in activism that lacks genuine commitment, often reducing complex issues to mere hashtags or slogans. This performative nature can dilute the message of authenticity, as it prioritizes visibility over substantive change. Lysa's approach to activism emphasizes the importance of genuine engagement, advocating for a movement that is rooted in lived experiences rather than performative gestures.

Examples of Authenticity in Activism

Lysa Wren's activism exemplifies the transformative power of authenticity. By openly sharing her journey of self-discovery, she has inspired countless individuals to embrace their identities unapologetically. One notable instance occurred during a public speaking engagement where Lysa discussed her struggles with self-acceptance. Her vulnerability resonated with the audience, fostering a sense of community and encouraging others to share their stories. This act of authenticity not only empowered individuals but also created a ripple effect, promoting dialogue about the importance of self-acceptance within the broader LGBTQ community.

Furthermore, Lysa's literary contributions, including poetry and essays, serve as a testament to the power of authentic expression. Her writings often reflect the complexities of identity, exploring themes of love, loss, and resilience. By articulating her experiences, she provides a platform for others to confront their own narratives, reinforcing the notion that authenticity is a collective journey rather than an isolated endeavor.

The Role of Authenticity in Societal Change

Authenticity plays a pivotal role in driving societal change. When individuals embrace their true selves, they challenge the status quo, prompting others to question their own assumptions about gender and sexuality. Lysa Wren's advocacy work, characterized by her unapologetic authenticity, has contributed to a cultural shift in Velmar. Her efforts to promote inclusive language and destigmatize gender non-conformity have encouraged individuals to express themselves freely, fostering a more accepting environment.

Moreover, the visibility of authentic voices in the LGBTQ community has catalyzed broader conversations about intersectionality and inclusivity. By acknowledging the diverse experiences within the community, activists can advocate for policies that reflect the needs of all individuals, regardless of their gender identity or sexual orientation. Lysa's commitment to intersectional activism reinforces the idea that authenticity is not only about personal expression but also about collective empowerment.

Conclusion

In conclusion, the importance of authenticity in LGBTQ activism cannot be overstated. Lysa Wren's journey serves as a powerful reminder that embracing one's true self is essential for personal growth and societal change. By challenging societal norms and advocating for inclusivity, Lysa exemplifies the transformative potential of authenticity. As the movement continues to evolve, fostering a culture of authenticity will be crucial in ensuring that all voices are heard and valued, paving the way for a more equitable future.

Setting the Stage for Change

In the vibrant tapestry of Velmar, where tradition often clashes with the burgeoning quest for authenticity, Lysa Wren emerged as a beacon of hope and change. The journey toward societal transformation is rarely linear; it is a complex interplay of individual courage, collective action, and the relentless pursuit of justice. Lysa understood that to set the stage for change, one must first dismantle the barriers that uphold systemic inequalities.

Theoretical Frameworks

To comprehend the dynamics of change, it is essential to explore various theoretical frameworks that inform LGBTQ activism. One such framework is *Queer Theory*, which challenges the binary understanding of gender and sexuality. Queer Theory posits that identities are fluid and socially constructed, urging activists to question normative assumptions. Lysa's activism was deeply rooted in these principles, advocating for a world where identities could flourish beyond rigid confines.

Another relevant theory is *Intersectionality*, coined by Kimberlé Crenshaw. This concept emphasizes that individuals experience overlapping social identities, leading to unique forms of discrimination and privilege. Lysa's approach to activism was inherently intersectional, recognizing that the fight for LGBTQ rights must also encompass issues of race, class, and disability. By integrating these theories into her work, Lysa laid the groundwork for a more inclusive movement.

Identifying Problems

Setting the stage for change requires a thorough understanding of the problems at hand. In Velmar, entrenched gender norms perpetuated discrimination, marginalizing those who dared to defy societal expectations. Lysa identified key issues, such as:

- **Lack of Representation:** Media and political landscapes often overlooked LGBTQ voices, leading to a skewed narrative that failed to capture the diversity of experiences.

- **Discrimination in Employment:** Many individuals faced unjust termination or hiring practices based on their sexual orientation or gender identity.

- **Healthcare Inequities:** Access to healthcare was fraught with challenges, particularly for transgender individuals seeking gender-affirming treatments.

- **Education Barriers:** Schools often lacked comprehensive LGBTQ-inclusive curricula, fostering environments of ignorance and intolerance.

By addressing these issues, Lysa aimed to create a comprehensive strategy for change, engaging allies and advocates from various sectors.

Examples of Activism

Lysa's activism was not merely theoretical; it manifested in tangible actions that galvanized the community. One notable campaign was the *Proud & Unapologetic* initiative, which sought to amplify LGBTQ voices through storytelling. By organizing workshops and open mic events, Lysa provided a platform for individuals to share their experiences, fostering a sense of solidarity and empowerment.

Additionally, Lysa spearheaded the *Velmar Pride March*, which became an annual event celebrating diversity and resilience. This march not only raised awareness but also served as a powerful demonstration of unity against oppression. The visibility generated by such events was crucial in challenging stereotypes and promoting acceptance within the broader community.

Creating Alliances

A pivotal aspect of setting the stage for change was Lysa's ability to forge alliances across various movements. Recognizing the interconnectedness of struggles, she collaborated with feminist groups, racial justice organizations, and disability advocates. This intersectional approach not only strengthened the LGBTQ movement but also enriched the dialogue surrounding social justice.

For instance, Lysa organized a panel discussion titled *"Unity in Diversity: A Call to Action"*, where activists from different backgrounds shared their experiences and strategies for advocacy. This event highlighted the importance of solidarity and collective action in the pursuit of equity.

The Role of Education

Education played a transformative role in Lysa's activism. By prioritizing awareness and understanding, she aimed to dismantle ignorance that often fuels discrimination. Lysa initiated educational programs in schools, focusing on

LGBTQ history, rights, and the importance of inclusivity. These programs not only educated students but also equipped teachers with the tools to foster supportive environments.

Furthermore, Lysa utilized social media as a powerful educational platform. Through engaging content, she challenged misconceptions and provided resources for those seeking to learn more about LGBTQ issues. Her ability to connect with a diverse audience was instrumental in spreading awareness and fostering dialogue.

Conclusion

Setting the stage for change is a multifaceted endeavor that requires a deep understanding of societal dynamics, a commitment to inclusivity, and the courage to challenge the status quo. Lysa Wren's journey exemplifies the power of activism rooted in theory, empathy, and collaboration. As she continued to advocate for a more equitable Velmar, her unfiltered voice resonated with many, inspiring a generation to embrace authenticity and fight for justice. The stage was set, and the movement was just beginning.

A Fearless Voice Emerges

The Power of Self-Education

Lysa Wren's Literary Influence

Lysa Wren's literary journey is a tapestry woven from threads of diverse influences, each contributing to her unique perspective on gender and identity. Growing up in Velmar, a place where traditional narratives often overshadowed emerging voices, Lysa found solace and empowerment in literature. Books became her refuge, offering her a glimpse into worlds where the constraints of gender norms could be challenged and redefined.

The Power of Words

Words hold immense power; they can uplift, challenge, and inspire. Lysa discovered this truth early on, as she immersed herself in the works of authors who dared to question societal expectations. Among her literary influences, the works of Virginia Woolf and James Baldwin stood out prominently. Woolf's exploration of gender fluidity and identity in *Orlando* resonated deeply with Lysa. Woolf's ability to transcend the confines of gender through her narrative style provided Lysa with a blueprint for her own writing, encouraging her to embrace the complexity of her identity.

James Baldwin's poignant essays on race, sexuality, and identity further shaped Lysa's understanding of intersectionality. Baldwin's fearless examination of societal issues inspired Lysa to confront the realities of discrimination and prejudice within her community. His assertion that "not everything that is faced can be changed, but nothing can be changed until it is faced" became a mantra for her activism. This literary influence instilled in Lysa the courage to voice her truths and advocate for change.

The Role of Poetry

In addition to prose, poetry played a pivotal role in Lysa's literary development. The works of Audre Lorde and Rainer Maria Rilke provided her with the language to articulate her experiences and emotions. Lorde's powerful verses on identity and self-acceptance resonated with Lysa's own struggles. Lorde's declaration that "the master's tools will never dismantle the master's house" became a guiding principle for Lysa, emphasizing the need for authentic voices in the fight for equality.

Rilke's exploration of existential themes and the human condition also influenced Lysa's writing. His poem "Letters to a Young Poet" encouraged her to embrace vulnerability and introspection, reminding her that self-discovery is a lifelong journey. This poetic influence encouraged Lysa to infuse her activism with a sense of artistry, using her words as a means of connection and understanding.

Creating a Literary Movement

As Lysa's literary influences began to coalesce, she felt a calling to create a movement that resonated with her experiences and those of others in Velmar. This desire led to the establishment of the "Proud & Unapologetic" movement, a platform where individuals could share their stories and express their identities without fear of judgment. The movement drew inspiration from the literary works that had shaped Lysa, emphasizing the importance of storytelling in the fight for acceptance.

Through workshops, readings, and community events, Lysa encouraged others to explore their own literary influences and share their narratives. This initiative not only fostered a sense of belonging but also highlighted the power of literature as a catalyst for change. Lysa understood that by amplifying diverse voices, she could challenge the status quo and promote a more inclusive society.

The Intersection of Literature and Activism

Lysa Wren's literary influences extend beyond mere inspiration; they form the foundation of her activism. By intertwining literature with her advocacy, she created a multifaceted approach to challenging gender norms. Lysa often quotes the feminist theorist bell hooks, who stated, "Life-transforming ideas have always come to me through books." This sentiment encapsulates Lysa's belief in the transformative power of literature.

In her speeches and writings, Lysa frequently references literary works to illustrate her points, using quotes and passages as tools to engage her audience. This approach not only enriches her message but also invites others to explore the literature that has shaped her journey. By doing so, Lysa encourages a dialogue that transcends the boundaries of gender and identity, fostering empathy and understanding within her community.

Conclusion

Lysa Wren's literary influences are a testament to the profound impact that literature can have on personal and societal transformation. Through her exploration of diverse voices and narratives, Lysa has cultivated a unique perspective on LGBTQ activism that challenges conventional norms. As she continues to draw inspiration from the literary world, Lysa remains committed to using her voice to advocate for change, ensuring that the stories of marginalized individuals are heard and celebrated. In doing so, she not only honors the authors who have shaped her journey but also paves the way for future generations of activists to find their own literary influences and make their mark on the world.

The Books That Shaped Her Thinking

Lysa Wren's intellectual journey was profoundly influenced by a diverse array of literature that challenged societal norms and encouraged critical thinking. Her reading list was not merely a collection of titles; it was a curated selection of texts that sparked her activism and shaped her identity.

Foundational Texts in Gender Studies

One of the cornerstones of Lysa's understanding of gender was Judith Butler's *Gender Trouble*. Butler's theory of gender performativity posits that gender is not an inherent quality but rather a series of acts and behaviors that are socially constructed. This idea resonated deeply with Lysa, who began to see her own experiences as part of a larger societal performance. Butler's assertion that *"gender is a kind of persistent impersonation that passes as the real"* challenged Lysa to deconstruct her own identity and the roles imposed upon her by society.

Queer Theory and Intersectionality

In addition to Butler, Lysa found inspiration in the works of bell hooks, particularly *Ain't I a Woman?*. Hooks's exploration of race, gender, and class provided Lysa with a framework for understanding the intersectionality of her activism. Hooks argued that *"the most profound and enduring change happens when we confront the intersecting systems of oppression"*, a perspective that encouraged Lysa to advocate for inclusivity within the LGBTQ community. This intersectional lens allowed her to address the unique struggles faced by individuals at the crossroads of multiple marginalized identities.

Literature as a Tool for Empathy

Lysa's literary journey also included reading works of fiction that illuminated the human experience. Books such as *Orlando* by Virginia Woolf and *The Color Purple* by Alice Walker expanded her understanding of gender fluidity and the complexities of identity. Woolf's exploration of time and gender through the character of Orlando challenged Lysa to think beyond binary constructs, while Walker's portrayal of resilience in the face of oppression inspired her to advocate for marginalized voices within her community.

The Power of Poetry

Poetry also played a significant role in Lysa's development as an activist. The works of poets like Audre Lorde and Rumi provided her with a means of expressing her emotions and struggles. Lorde's powerful declaration that *"the master's tools will never dismantle the master's house"* became a rallying cry for Lysa, emphasizing the need for radical change rather than mere reform. Rumi's spiritual insights encouraged her to embrace love and compassion as essential components of her activism.

Engaging with Contemporary Voices

As Lysa's activism evolved, she began to engage with contemporary authors such as Roxane Gay and Chimamanda Ngozi Adichie. Gay's *Bad Feminist* offered a nuanced perspective on feminism, allowing Lysa to embrace the complexities of her own identity without the pressure of perfection. Adichie's famous TED talk, *We Should All Be Feminists*, provided Lysa with a modern context for her activism, reinforcing the importance of inclusivity and understanding in the fight for gender equality.

The Role of Non-Fiction

Non-fiction works, particularly those focused on LGBTQ history and rights, also shaped Lysa's activism. Books like *The Gay Revolution* by Lillian Faderman and *Queer (In)Justice* by Joey L. Mogul, Andrea J. Ritchie, and Kay Whitlock offered Lysa a historical perspective on the struggles faced by the LGBTQ community. Faderman's documentation of the fight for gay rights illustrated the progress made and the battles yet to be fought, while Mogul et al. highlighted the intersections of race, gender, and sexuality within the justice system.

Conclusion

Through her extensive reading, Lysa Wren cultivated a rich understanding of gender, identity, and activism. The books she encountered not only informed her theoretical framework but also provided her with the tools to navigate the complexities of her own identity. By engaging with a diverse range of voices and perspectives, Lysa was able to forge a unique path in her activism, one that embraced authenticity, empathy, and a commitment to challenging the status quo. As she continued her journey, the lessons gleaned from these texts remained integral to her mission of breaking down gender norms and advocating for a more inclusive society.

From Poetry to Prose: Lysa Wren's Writing Journey

Lysa Wren's evolution as a writer is a testament to her journey of self-discovery and activism. Initially, she expressed her thoughts and emotions through poetry, using the medium as a refuge and a means of articulating the complexities of her identity. Poetry allowed Lysa to explore her inner world, weaving together the threads of her experiences with gender norms and societal expectations.

The Role of Poetry in Self-Expression

Poetry, with its inherent brevity and emotional resonance, served as a powerful tool for Lysa. It provided her a platform to voice her struggles, joys, and revelations. As she penned verses that reflected her experiences in Velmar, she found solace in the rhythm of her words. The act of writing poetry became a cathartic experience, allowing her to confront her internalized fears and societal pressures.

For example, one of her early poems, *"In the Mirror"*, captures the conflict between her perceived identity and her true self:

> *In the mirror, a stranger stares,*
> *Clad in armor of expectations,*
> *A heart beating, yet bound by chains,*
> *Yearning to break free, to be seen.*

This poem encapsulates the essence of her struggle, illustrating the disconnect between societal norms and her authentic self.

Transitioning to Prose

As Lysa's confidence grew, so did her desire to delve deeper into the narratives surrounding her identity and activism. She began to transition from poetry to prose, recognizing that prose offered a broader canvas to explore complex themes. Writing essays and personal narratives allowed her to dissect the intricacies of gender identity, societal expectations, and the LGBTQ experience in Velmar.

Lysa's prose was characterized by its raw honesty and vulnerability. She often drew from her poetic roots, infusing her essays with lyrical language that resonated with readers. Her transition was not without challenges; she grappled with the fear of losing the emotional depth that poetry provided. However, she soon realized that prose could also evoke powerful emotions through storytelling.

Thematic Exploration in Prose

In her prose works, Lysa tackled themes such as identity, acceptance, and the fight against discrimination. One notable essay, *"Beyond the Binary"*, explores the limitations of traditional gender constructs and advocates for a more inclusive understanding of identity. In it, she writes:

> Gender is not a binary; it is a spectrum,
> A kaleidoscope of identities,
> Each hue vibrant, each story valid,
> We must embrace the fluidity of our existence.

This essay not only reflects her personal journey but also serves as a rallying cry for others to embrace their authentic selves.

Influence of Literary Figures

Lysa's writing journey was significantly influenced by literary figures who challenged societal norms. Writers such as Audre Lorde, James Baldwin, and Virginia Woolf inspired her to weave her narrative into the larger tapestry of LGBTQ literature. Their works provided her with a framework for understanding her own experiences and the importance of representation in literature.

Lysa often cited Lorde's concept of the "erotic" as a source of empowerment, encouraging her to embrace her desires and experiences as valid and worthy of exploration. This influence is evident in her writing, where she often intertwines personal anecdotes with broader societal critiques.

The Birth of a Unique Voice

As Lysa honed her craft, she developed a unique voice that resonated with readers both within and outside the LGBTQ community. Her ability to articulate the nuances of her experiences allowed her to connect with a diverse audience. Through public readings and online platforms, she shared her prose, fostering dialogue around gender identity and activism.

Lysa's writing became a vehicle for change, inspiring others to share their stories and challenge societal norms. Her journey from poetry to prose exemplifies the transformative power of writing as a tool for self-discovery and activism.

Conclusion: A Journey of Growth

Lysa Wren's writing journey reflects her growth as an individual and an activist. From the intimate expressions of her poetry to the expansive narratives of her prose, she has carved a space for herself in the literary world. Her work continues to inspire others to embrace their identities and challenge the status quo, proving that the written word can be a catalyst for change.

In her own words, she encapsulates her journey:

> *Through every line, I found my truth,*
> *In every stanza, a piece of my soul,*
> *From poetry to prose, I learned to fight,*
> *For love, for freedom, for the right to be whole.*

Lysa Wren's literary journey is a testament to the power of words in shaping identities and fostering understanding, leaving an indelible mark on the landscape of LGBTQ activism and literature.

The Evolution of Her Activism

Lysa Wren's activism did not emerge in a vacuum; it was a dynamic response to the shifting landscapes of societal norms and the urgent calls for change within her community. The evolution of her activism can be understood through a series of transformative phases, each marked by significant theoretical insights, practical challenges, and impactful examples.

Theoretical Foundations

At the heart of Lysa's activism lies a profound understanding of intersectionality, a theory coined by Kimberlé Crenshaw in the late 1980s. Intersectionality posits that individuals experience overlapping systems of discrimination and privilege based on various aspects of their identity, including race, gender, sexuality, and class. This framework became a cornerstone of Lysa's approach, as she recognized that the fight for LGBTQ rights could not be separated from broader social justice movements.

Lysa often cited the work of bell hooks, who emphasized the importance of love and compassion in activism. This perspective encouraged her to cultivate a movement that was not only fierce in its demands but also nurturing in its approach. The combination of intersectionality and love as a guiding principle allowed Lysa to create an inclusive environment where diverse voices were heard and celebrated.

Early Activism: Grassroots Engagement

Initially, Lysa's activism took shape at the grassroots level. Inspired by her early experiences with discrimination, she organized small community meetings in Velmar, creating safe spaces for LGBTQ individuals to share their stories. These gatherings were characterized by an ethos of vulnerability and mutual support. The impact was palpable; participants often left feeling empowered and validated.

One notable event was the first "Pride in the Park" gathering, which Lysa organized in response to the lack of visible LGBTQ representation in Velmar. The event attracted a diverse crowd, including allies from various backgrounds, demonstrating the power of collective action. Lysa's ability to foster connections among different groups was pivotal in establishing a united front against discrimination.

Digital Activism: Harnessing Social Media

As Lysa's influence grew, she recognized the potential of digital platforms to amplify her message. The advent of social media provided an unprecedented opportunity to reach a wider audience. Lysa adeptly utilized platforms like Twitter and Instagram to share her insights, engage in dialogue, and mobilize support for various causes.

Her hashtag campaign, #ProudAndUnapologetic, quickly gained traction, encouraging individuals to share their stories of resilience and pride. This digital movement not only fostered a sense of community but also challenged the narratives perpetuated by mainstream media. Lysa's posts often combined personal anecdotes with calls to action, creating a blend of storytelling and activism that resonated deeply with her followers.

Confronting Challenges: Backlash and Resilience

With increased visibility came increased scrutiny. Lysa faced significant backlash from conservative factions within Velmar, including threats and derogatory comments aimed at her character and activism. However, rather than retreating, she leaned into the discomfort. Lysa often spoke about the importance of resilience in her activism, drawing from the teachings of Audre Lorde, who famously stated, "Your silence will not protect you."

Lysa's response to criticism was multifaceted. She organized community forums to address concerns and misconceptions about LGBTQ identities, fostering dialogue even in the face of hostility. By humanizing the issues and sharing personal narratives, she was able to dismantle some of the prejudices that fueled opposition.

Building Alliances: A Collaborative Approach

Recognizing that the fight for LGBTQ rights was interconnected with other social justice movements, Lysa actively sought to build alliances. She collaborated with feminist groups, racial justice organizations, and environmental activists, understanding that the liberation of one group is tied to the liberation of all.

One significant collaboration was with the local women's shelter, where Lysa led workshops on LGBTQ inclusivity and gender identity. This initiative not only educated staff but also provided a safe space for LGBTQ individuals seeking refuge. The partnership exemplified Lysa's commitment to intersectional activism, showcasing the importance of solidarity across movements.

Legacy of Activism: Inspiring Future Generations

As Lysa's activism evolved, so did her role as a mentor. She began to focus on empowering the next generation of activists, recognizing that sustainable change requires ongoing engagement. Through mentorship programs and workshops, Lysa instilled in young activists the importance of authenticity and self-advocacy.

Her influence extended beyond Velmar, as she became a sought-after speaker at national conferences and events. Lysa's ability to articulate the nuances of LGBTQ activism, grounded in personal experience and theoretical understanding, inspired many to carry the torch of advocacy forward.

Conclusion: A Continuous Journey

The evolution of Lysa Wren's activism is a testament to her adaptability, resilience, and unwavering commitment to justice. From grassroots organizing to digital activism and collaborative efforts, her journey reflects the complexities of fighting for LGBTQ rights in a world that often resists change. As she continues to challenge the status quo, Lysa remains an unfiltered voice for authenticity, inclusivity, and love, inspiring countless individuals to embrace their identities and advocate for a more equitable society.

Engaging With Other Activists

Lysa Wren's journey as an LGBTQ activist was not a solitary one; it was deeply intertwined with the vibrant tapestry of voices that make up the broader movement. Engaging with other activists became a cornerstone of her approach, allowing her to amplify her message and cultivate a sense of community. This section explores the dynamics of her collaborations, the theoretical underpinnings of collective activism, and the challenges that arise when diverse voices come together for a common cause.

Theoretical Framework

At the heart of Lysa's engagement with fellow activists lies the theory of *collective efficacy*, which posits that individuals working together toward a common goal can achieve greater outcomes than they could alone. According to Bandura (1997), collective efficacy is built on shared beliefs in the ability of a group to organize and execute actions required to achieve desired outcomes. For Lysa, this meant recognizing that her individual experiences were part of a larger narrative, one that could be enriched through collaboration.

Building Alliances

Lysa understood that forming alliances with other activists was essential for creating a more inclusive movement. She actively sought out partnerships with groups that represented a spectrum of identities, including racial minorities, the disabled, and those from various socio-economic backgrounds. This intersectional approach not only broadened her perspective but also enriched the dialogue around LGBTQ issues.

For instance, during the planning of the "Proud & Unapologetic" movement, Lysa collaborated with activists from the Black Lives Matter movement to address the unique challenges faced by LGBTQ people of color. This collaboration not only highlighted the intersections of race and sexuality but also emphasized the importance of acknowledging and addressing systemic oppression in all its forms.

Challenges in Collaboration

While Lysa's efforts to engage with other activists were largely fruitful, they were not without challenges. One significant issue was the potential for *tokenism*, where marginalized voices are included in discussions but not given the platform or respect they deserve. Lysa was acutely aware of this danger and worked diligently to ensure that all voices were not only heard but valued.

Moreover, differences in priorities and methodologies among activists could lead to friction. For example, some activists advocated for more radical approaches, while others favored legislative reform. Lysa navigated these differences by fostering open dialogues, encouraging each group to articulate their perspectives and find common ground. This approach not only mitigated conflicts but also enriched the movement's strategies.

Examples of Engagement

One notable example of Lysa's engagement with other activists occurred during the annual Velmar Pride Festival. Lysa organized a panel discussion featuring representatives from various activist groups, including transgender rights advocates, mental health professionals, and intersectional feminists. The panel's diverse perspectives allowed for a rich discussion on the complexities of identity and the multifaceted nature of oppression.

Additionally, Lysa utilized social media as a tool for engagement. She created a series of online discussions that brought together activists from different regions and backgrounds to share their experiences and strategies. This virtual platform allowed for the exchange of ideas and fostered a sense of solidarity among activists who might otherwise feel isolated in their own communities.

The Role of Mentorship

Lysa also recognized the importance of mentorship in activist engagement. By connecting with seasoned activists, she was able to gain insights into effective strategies and the historical context of the LGBTQ movement. This mentorship not only informed her approach but also helped her to mentor emerging activists, creating a cycle of knowledge sharing that strengthened the movement as a whole.

For instance, Lysa's relationship with veteran activist Marisol Rivera proved pivotal. Marisol's experience in grassroots organizing provided Lysa with the tools to mobilize her community effectively. Together, they launched initiatives that addressed local issues, such as homelessness among LGBTQ youth, demonstrating the power of mentorship in fostering new leadership.

Conclusion

Engaging with other activists was a transformative aspect of Lysa Wren's journey. By building alliances, navigating challenges, and fostering mentorship, she not only amplified her own voice but also contributed to a more inclusive and effective LGBTQ movement. Through her commitment to collaboration, Lysa demonstrated that the fight for equality is not just an individual endeavor but a collective struggle that thrives on diversity, empathy, and shared purpose.

The Birth of the "Proud & Unapologetic" Movement

The emergence of the "Proud & Unapologetic" movement marked a pivotal moment in Lysa Wren's activism, serving as a clarion call for authenticity and self-acceptance within the LGBTQ community. This movement was not merely a reaction to societal pressures; it was a profound declaration of identity, rooted in the understanding that visibility and pride are essential to dismantling the barriers imposed by heteronormative standards.

Theoretical Foundations

At the core of the "Proud & Unapologetic" movement lies the theory of intersectionality, which posits that various social categorizations, such as race, gender, and sexual orientation, intersect to create overlapping systems of discrimination or disadvantage. This framework was essential for Lysa Wren as she sought to create an inclusive space that acknowledged the diverse experiences within the LGBTQ community.

The movement also drew upon Judith Butler's concept of gender performativity, which asserts that gender is not an innate quality but rather a series of acts and behaviors that individuals perform. Wren's advocacy encouraged individuals to embrace their unique expressions of gender and sexuality, thereby challenging the rigid binaries that have historically constrained identities.

Addressing Problems

Despite its noble intentions, the "Proud & Unapologetic" movement faced significant challenges. One primary obstacle was the backlash from conservative factions that viewed the movement as a threat to traditional values. This resistance often manifested in derogatory rhetoric and attempts to undermine the legitimacy of LGBTQ identities.

Moreover, within the LGBTQ community itself, there were divisions regarding the movement's approach. Some critics argued that the emphasis on pride could inadvertently alienate those who were not yet comfortable expressing their identities publicly. Wren addressed these concerns by emphasizing the importance of self-acceptance, stating, "Pride is not a uniform experience; it is a spectrum that must be respected."

Examples of Impact

The impact of the "Proud & Unapologetic" movement can be seen in various initiatives that emerged under its banner. One notable example was the "Pride in Diversity" campaign, which aimed to highlight the stories of LGBTQ individuals from different backgrounds. Through a series of workshops and social media campaigns, participants shared their narratives, fostering a sense of community and solidarity.

Additionally, the movement inspired the creation of safe spaces in schools and workplaces, where individuals could express their identities without fear of discrimination. These spaces became incubators for dialogue, allowing for the exploration of complex issues such as gender fluidity and non-binary identities.

A Call to Action

The "Proud & Unapologetic" movement also served as a rallying point for activism. It called upon individuals to engage in advocacy work, whether through grassroots organizing, participating in pride parades, or simply sharing their stories. Wren famously stated, "Your voice is your power. Use it unapologetically." This mantra resonated with many, galvanizing a new generation of activists who were eager to challenge the status quo.

Conclusion

In conclusion, the birth of the "Proud & Unapologetic" movement represented a significant evolution in LGBTQ activism, emphasizing the necessity of authenticity and intersectionality. Through Lysa Wren's leadership, the movement not only challenged existing gender norms but also empowered individuals to embrace their identities fully. As the movement continues to grow, it remains a testament to the power of pride, resilience, and unapologetic self-expression in the ongoing fight for equality.

Navigating Social Media Fame

In the digital age, social media has emerged as a double-edged sword for activists like Lysa Wren. While it provides a platform for amplifying voices and fostering community, it also exposes individuals to scrutiny and backlash. Lysa's rise to prominence on various social media platforms exemplifies the complexities of navigating fame in an era where every post can spark a conversation—or controversy.

The Power of Social Media

Social media platforms such as Twitter, Instagram, and TikTok have revolutionized the way activists communicate their messages. For Lysa, these platforms were not merely tools for self-promotion; they became vital spaces for dialogue and activism. The immediacy of social media allowed her to share her thoughts on gender norms and LGBTQ issues in real-time, reaching a global audience. As noted by theorist [?], social media acts as a "networked public sphere," where marginalized voices can challenge dominant narratives.

Crafting a Persona

Lysa Wren's social media presence was carefully curated to reflect her values and mission. She embraced authenticity, sharing personal stories that resonated with her followers. This approach aligns with the concept of *performative identity* as discussed by [?], where individuals express their identities through repeated actions that conform to societal expectations. Lysa's posts often included hashtags like #ProudAndUnapologetic, creating a brand that encapsulated her activism while encouraging others to embrace their identities.

Engagement and Community Building

Through her engaging content, Lysa fostered a sense of community among her followers. She utilized interactive features such as polls, Q&A sessions, and live discussions to encourage dialogue. This strategy reflects the participatory culture described by [?], where audiences are not passive consumers but active participants in the creation of content. By valuing her followers' input, Lysa cultivated a supportive environment that empowered individuals to share their experiences and challenges.

Facing Backlash and Criticism

However, the visibility that comes with social media fame is not without its challenges. Lysa faced significant backlash from conservative factions and individuals who opposed her views. Cyberbullying, targeted harassment, and misinformation became part of her reality. This phenomenon is supported by the *spiral of silence* theory proposed by [?], which suggests that individuals may refrain from expressing dissenting opinions due to fear of social isolation. Lysa's resilience in the face of adversity showcased her commitment to her cause, as she often addressed criticism head-on while maintaining her authenticity.

Navigating Mental Health Challenges

The pressures of social media fame also took a toll on Lysa's mental health. The constant scrutiny and the need to maintain a public persona led to feelings of anxiety and self-doubt. According to [?], the correlation between social media use and mental health issues is well-documented, particularly among young activists. Lysa recognized the importance of self-care and sought therapy to navigate these challenges. She often shared her journey with her followers, emphasizing the significance of mental health awareness within the LGBTQ community.

Leveraging Social Media for Advocacy

Despite the challenges, Lysa adeptly leveraged her social media presence for advocacy. She organized campaigns, collaborated with other activists, and raised funds for LGBTQ organizations through her platforms. The effectiveness of social media in mobilizing support is illustrated by the success of the #BlackLivesMatter movement, which utilized platforms to raise awareness and incite action. Lysa's campaigns mirrored this model, demonstrating the potential of social media as a catalyst for change.

The Future of Activism in the Digital Age

As Lysa Wren continued to navigate her social media fame, she became acutely aware of the evolving landscape of digital activism. The rise of new platforms and the changing algorithms of existing ones meant that adaptability was crucial. Lysa's journey serves as a case study in the need for activists to remain agile, embracing new technologies while staying true to their core messages. The concept of *digital resilience*, as discussed by [?], emphasizes the importance of maintaining one's voice amid the challenges posed by the digital environment.

In conclusion, Lysa Wren's navigation of social media fame illustrates the intricate balance between visibility and vulnerability. While social media offers unprecedented opportunities for connection and advocacy, it also presents significant challenges that activists must confront. Lysa's experience serves as a reminder of the power of authenticity, community, and resilience in the ever-evolving landscape of digital activism.

A Platform for Dialogue and Progress

In an era defined by rapid social change and evolving norms, Lysa Wren emerged as a fearless advocate for LGBTQ rights, leveraging her platform to foster dialogue and promote progressive ideals. The significance of dialogue in activism cannot be overstated; it serves as the bedrock upon which understanding, empathy, and collaboration are built. Lysa recognized early on that to effect meaningful change, it was essential to create spaces where diverse voices could be heard and where the complexities of identity could be explored openly.

The Role of Dialogue in Activism

At the heart of Lysa's activism was the belief that dialogue is not merely a tool but a transformative process that can bridge divides. As theorized by Paulo Freire in his seminal work, *Pedagogy of the Oppressed*, dialogue fosters critical consciousness and empowers individuals to reflect on their realities. Freire posits that through dialogue, oppressed individuals can reclaim their narrative and challenge oppressive structures. Lysa adopted this philosophy, organizing workshops and community forums that encouraged participants to share their experiences and perspectives on gender and sexuality.

In these forums, Lysa employed the concept of *intersectionality*, coined by Kimberlé Crenshaw, to illustrate how various identities intersect and impact individuals' lived experiences. By acknowledging the interconnectedness of race, gender, class, and sexuality, Lysa facilitated discussions that highlighted the unique struggles faced by marginalized communities within the LGBTQ spectrum. This approach not only enriched the dialogue but also fostered a sense of solidarity among participants.

The Challenges of Dialogue

Despite its potential, fostering dialogue in a polarized environment is fraught with challenges. Lysa encountered resistance from individuals entrenched in traditional gender norms who viewed her ideas as threatening. This backlash is not uncommon in social movements, as noted by social theorist Charles Tilly, who argues that movements often face opposition from established power structures seeking to maintain the status quo.

To counteract this resistance, Lysa emphasized the importance of *active listening*—a practice that involves not only hearing but also understanding and valuing differing viewpoints. She often cited the work of Marshall Rosenberg, whose principles of Nonviolent Communication advocate for empathetic engagement as a means to resolve conflict and promote understanding. By modeling active listening in her interactions, Lysa was able to create a more inclusive atmosphere, encouraging even the most skeptical participants to engage in constructive dialogue.

Examples of Dialogue in Action

One of the most impactful initiatives led by Lysa was the establishment of the *Proud & Unapologetic* roundtable discussions, which brought together activists, educators, and community members to discuss pressing issues facing the LGBTQ community in Velmar. These gatherings became a crucible for ideas, where participants shared personal stories, debated strategies, and collaboratively developed action plans.

During one particularly poignant session, a participant shared their experience of navigating the healthcare system as a non-binary individual. This story resonated deeply with others in the room, sparking a discussion about the systemic barriers faced by gender non-conforming individuals in accessing medical care. As a result, the group formulated a campaign aimed at advocating for inclusive healthcare policies, illustrating how dialogue can lead to tangible action.

Additionally, Lysa utilized social media as a platform for dialogue, recognizing its power to reach a broader audience. By hosting live discussions and Q&A sessions, she engaged with followers from diverse backgrounds, allowing for real-time exchanges of ideas. This digital outreach not only amplified marginalized voices but also democratized the conversation around LGBTQ issues, making it accessible to those who might not have been able to participate in traditional forums.

The Impact of Dialogue on Progress

The impact of Lysa's commitment to dialogue was profound. By fostering an environment of open communication, she was able to dismantle misconceptions and build bridges between disparate groups. As documented in the research of social psychologist Henri Tajfel, intergroup dialogue can reduce prejudice and promote understanding among conflicting parties. Lysa's initiatives exemplified this principle, as many participants reported a shift in their perspectives and an increased willingness to advocate for LGBTQ rights.

Moreover, the dialogues initiated by Lysa contributed to a culture of accountability within the Velmar community. Participants learned to recognize their biases and engage in self-reflection, ultimately leading to a more inclusive and supportive environment for all individuals, regardless of their gender identity or sexual orientation. This cultural shift is crucial for sustaining progress, as it empowers community members to hold each other accountable and advocate for systemic change.

In conclusion, Lysa Wren's dedication to creating a platform for dialogue and progress has left an indelible mark on Velmar's LGBTQ activism landscape. Through her efforts, she not only challenged existing norms but also cultivated a culture of understanding and empathy that continues to inspire future generations. As we reflect on her journey, it becomes evident that dialogue is not just a means to an end; it is the very essence of activism, paving the way for a more equitable and inclusive society.

Facing Backlash and Criticism

As Lysa Wren's voice grew louder in the realm of LGBTQ activism, so too did the cacophony of dissent that often accompanies those who dare to challenge societal norms. The backlash she faced was multi-faceted, stemming from various sectors of society that felt threatened by her unfiltered approach to activism. This section delves into the nature of this criticism, the theories behind societal backlash, and the strategies Lysa employed to navigate these turbulent waters.

The Nature of Backlash

Backlash against LGBTQ activism is not a new phenomenon; it is deeply rooted in historical resistance to change. Theories such as *social identity theory* (Tajfel & Turner, 1979) suggest that individuals derive part of their self-esteem from their group memberships. Consequently, when a marginalized group, such as the LGBTQ community, begins to assert its rights and identity, those who identify with the dominant group may react defensively to preserve their social status. Lysa's advocacy for non-binary identities, fluidity, and intersectionality posed a direct challenge to the rigid gender norms that many people clung to, igniting fear and hostility.

Examples of Backlash

Lysa's outspoken nature on platforms like social media often attracted a storm of criticism. For instance, her viral post discussing the importance of inclusive language in everyday discourse received significant backlash from conservative commentators, who accused her of attempting to "erase" traditional gender roles. This reaction was emblematic of the larger societal struggle between progressive and conservative ideologies regarding gender and sexuality.

Furthermore, Lysa faced personal attacks that targeted her identity and credibility. Critics would often dismiss her as an "attention seeker" or label her activism as "extreme." This dismissal is part of a broader phenomenon known as *delegitimization*, where the contributions of marginalized voices are minimized or invalidated. Lysa's response to such criticism was not to retreat but to engage, often using her platform to articulate the importance of diverse perspectives in activism.

Theoretical Frameworks Behind Criticism

Understanding the backlash Lysa faced also requires an examination of *cognitive dissonance theory* (Festinger, 1957). This theory posits that when individuals are confronted with information that contradicts their beliefs, they experience psychological discomfort, leading them to rationalize or dismiss the new information. Lysa's advocacy for fluidity and non-binary identities clashed with the binary mindset of many, resulting in a defensive backlash as individuals sought to maintain their existing beliefs.

Moreover, the concept of *intersectionality* (Crenshaw, 1989) plays a crucial role in understanding the complexity of backlash. Lysa's activism was not only about gender identity but also about race, class, and sexuality, which compounded the criticism she faced. For instance, her emphasis on the experiences of transgender individuals of color drew ire from some within the LGBTQ community who felt that their struggles were being overshadowed. This illustrates the internal conflicts within activist movements, where differing priorities can lead to criticism from within and outside the community.

Strategies for Navigating Backlash

In the face of such criticism, Lysa employed several strategies to maintain her focus and continue her advocacy. One key approach was *reframing*, a technique used to shift the narrative surrounding her activism. Instead of viewing criticism as a personal attack, Lysa framed it as an opportunity for dialogue and education. She often responded to detractors with well-researched arguments, providing evidence and personal anecdotes that highlighted the importance of her message.

Additionally, Lysa sought support from her allies within the activist community. Forming coalitions with other marginalized groups allowed her to amplify her voice and create a united front against criticism. This strategy not only provided her with emotional support but also strengthened her message through collective action.

The Role of Resilience

Resilience emerged as a key theme in Lysa's response to backlash. Psychological research indicates that resilience is crucial for individuals facing adversity, allowing them to bounce back from challenges and continue pursuing their goals (Masten, 2001). Lysa's ability to remain steadfast in her convictions, despite the negativity she encountered, served as an inspiration to many within the LGBTQ community. Her journey exemplified the idea that facing criticism is often an integral part of the path toward meaningful change.

Conclusion: The Power of Dialogue

Ultimately, Lysa Wren's experience with backlash and criticism highlights the complex dynamics of activism in a polarized society. By understanding the underlying theories of social identity, cognitive dissonance, and intersectionality, we can better appreciate the challenges faced by those who advocate for change. Lysa's unwavering commitment to her cause, coupled with her strategies for navigating criticism, serves as a powerful reminder of the importance of dialogue and resilience in the ongoing fight for LGBTQ rights. In this way, she not only challenged the status quo but also fostered a more inclusive conversation about identity and acceptance in Velmar and beyond.

Staying True to Her Message

In the ever-evolving landscape of LGBTQ activism, maintaining authenticity can often feel like navigating a labyrinth. For Lysa Wren, staying true to her message was not merely a personal ethos but a necessary compass guiding her through the complexities of public life and activism. The essence of her message centered on inclusivity, self-acceptance, and the dismantling of harmful stereotypes, which she articulated with unwavering conviction.

Theoretical Underpinnings

Lysa's approach draws upon the theory of *intersectionality*, as introduced by Kimberlé Crenshaw. This framework emphasizes that individuals experience oppression in varying configurations and degrees of intensity based on multiple aspects of their identities, including race, gender, and sexual orientation. Lysa understood that to remain true to her message, she had to advocate for a broad spectrum of identities within the LGBTQ community, recognizing that each voice contributed to a richer narrative.

Challenges Faced

However, Lysa's journey was not without its challenges. As her visibility increased, so did the scrutiny from various factions within and outside the LGBTQ community. Critics often accused her of being too radical or not radical enough, reflecting the paradox of activism where one can be both celebrated and vilified. This duality posed a significant challenge for Lysa, who grappled with the fear of alienating potential allies while striving to remain loyal to her core beliefs.

Navigating Backlash

Lysa faced backlash particularly when addressing issues like the representation of transgender individuals in mainstream media. For instance, in a viral social media post, she criticized a popular television show for its lack of authentic transgender representation, sparking a heated debate. While many praised her for speaking out, others accused her of being divisive. Lysa's response was rooted in her commitment to authenticity; she emphasized that her critique aimed to foster dialogue and encourage more accurate portrayals, rather than to silence dissenting voices.

Examples of Staying True

One poignant example of Lysa's commitment to her message occurred during the annual Velmar Pride Parade. In 2022, she delivered a speech that resonated deeply with attendees, emphasizing the importance of embracing one's identity without compromise. She stated, "We are not just a community; we are a tapestry woven from diverse threads. Each story matters, and together, we create a narrative that challenges the status quo." This moment exemplified her ability to connect with her audience while reinforcing her core principles.

The Role of Community Support

Lysa's steadfastness was bolstered by a network of allies and supporters who shared her vision. Through collaborative efforts, she organized workshops and discussions that allowed for open dialogue about identity and representation. This communal approach not only amplified her message but also fostered a sense of solidarity among participants, reinforcing the idea that activism is a collective endeavor.

Conclusion

Ultimately, Lysa Wren's journey exemplifies the delicate balance of staying true to one's message amid the cacophony of societal expectations and criticisms. By grounding her activism in the principles of intersectionality and community engagement, she has carved out a space that invites individuals to embrace their authentic selves. Her legacy serves as a reminder that in the pursuit of justice and equality, authenticity is not just a personal choice but a powerful tool for change.

$$\text{Authenticity} = \frac{\text{Self-Expression} + \text{Community Engagement}}{\text{Criticism} + \text{Visibility}} \tag{9}$$

In this equation, authenticity is depicted as a function of self-expression and community engagement, balanced against the challenges of criticism and visibility. This highlights that true activism thrives when individuals are empowered to express themselves while fostering connections with others who share their vision for a more inclusive society.

Breaking Down Gender Norms

Challenging Binary Constructs

Redefining Masculinity

In the contemporary discourse surrounding gender, the concept of masculinity is undergoing a profound transformation. Traditional notions of masculinity, often characterized by traits such as stoicism, aggression, and emotional suppression, are increasingly being challenged. This redefinition is crucial in the context of LGBTQ activism, as it opens the door for a broader understanding of gender and identity.

The Traditional Masculine Ideal

Historically, masculinity has been defined by a rigid set of norms. These norms dictate how men should behave, feel, and express themselves. The archetypal "man" is often seen as strong, unemotional, and dominant. This narrow definition not only marginalizes those who do not fit into this mold but also places immense pressure on individuals who identify as men to conform to these expectations.

The sociologist R.W. Connell introduced the concept of *hegemonic masculinity*, which refers to the dominant form of masculinity that is culturally exalted. Connell argues that this form of masculinity is characterized by the subordination of women and the marginalization of other masculinities, creating a hierarchy that reinforces gender inequality. The implications of hegemonic masculinity are pervasive, affecting interpersonal relationships and societal structures.

Challenging Traditional Norms

Lysa Wren's activism plays a pivotal role in challenging these traditional norms. By advocating for a more inclusive understanding of masculinity, she encourages individuals to embrace vulnerability, emotional expression, and nurturing qualities.

This shift is not merely about allowing men to express emotions; it is about dismantling the societal structures that dictate what it means to be a man.

One of the key theories that supports this redefinition is Judith Butler's concept of *gender performativity*. Butler posits that gender is not an inherent quality but rather a series of performances that individuals enact based on societal expectations. This perspective invites individuals to reconsider masculinity as a fluid construct rather than a fixed identity. By recognizing that masculinity can be performed in diverse ways, individuals can liberate themselves from the constraints of traditional norms.

Examples of Redefining Masculinity

Lysa's work exemplifies the redefinition of masculinity through various initiatives that promote diverse representations of male identities. For instance, she has collaborated with artists and activists to create campaigns that highlight the experiences of men who embrace non-traditional roles, such as stay-at-home fathers, caregivers, and men who engage in emotional labor. These campaigns challenge the stereotype that caregiving is solely a feminine trait, thereby expanding the definition of masculinity to include nurturing and supportive behaviors.

Moreover, Lysa has utilized social media platforms to amplify the voices of men who challenge traditional masculinity. Through her "Proud & Unapologetic" movement, she has created safe spaces for men to share their stories of vulnerability and self-discovery. This initiative not only fosters a sense of community but also encourages men to embrace their authentic selves without fear of judgment.

The Role of Intersectionality

An essential aspect of redefining masculinity is the recognition of intersectionality. Masculinity is not a monolithic experience; it is influenced by various factors, including race, class, sexuality, and culture. Lysa emphasizes the importance of understanding how these intersecting identities shape individual experiences of masculinity. For example, the experiences of a Black man navigating masculinity may differ significantly from those of a white man due to systemic racism and societal expectations.

By incorporating an intersectional lens, Lysa's activism highlights the diverse experiences of men within the LGBTQ community. She advocates for the inclusion of marginalized voices, recognizing that the redefinition of masculinity must encompass the complexities of identity and experience.

The Path Forward

As society continues to grapple with evolving gender norms, the redefinition of masculinity remains a critical aspect of LGBTQ activism. Lysa Wren's work serves as a beacon of hope, demonstrating that it is possible to challenge and redefine traditional constructs of masculinity.

The journey towards a more inclusive understanding of masculinity requires collective effort. It involves engaging in open dialogues, fostering empathy, and creating spaces where individuals can express their identities freely. By embracing a redefined masculinity that values emotional expression, vulnerability, and inclusivity, society can move closer to achieving true gender equality.

In conclusion, redefining masculinity is not merely an act of rebellion against traditional norms; it is a necessary step towards creating a more equitable and just society. Lysa Wren's activism exemplifies the power of challenging the status quo and advocating for a broader, more inclusive understanding of what it means to be a man in today's world.

Deconstructing Femininity

The concept of femininity has long been constructed through societal norms and expectations that dictate how individuals who identify as female should behave, dress, and express themselves. Lysa Wren, in her journey of activism, recognizes that these constructs are not only limiting but also harmful, perpetuating stereotypes that can lead to discrimination and exclusion. Deconstructing femininity involves critically analyzing these norms and challenging the binary notions of gender that confine individuals to rigid roles.

Theoretical Framework

The deconstruction of femininity draws heavily from feminist theory, particularly the works of Simone de Beauvoir, Judith Butler, and bell hooks. De Beauvoir's assertion that "one is not born, but rather becomes a woman" highlights the social construction of femininity, suggesting that gender is a performance shaped by cultural expectations rather than an innate quality. Judith Butler expands on this idea with her theory of gender performativity, which posits that gender is constituted through repeated actions and behaviors, thereby allowing for the possibility of subverting traditional gender roles.

$$G = P_1 + P_2 + P_3 + \ldots + P_n \tag{10}$$

Where G represents gender identity and P represents the various performances that contribute to the construction of that identity.

Challenging Norms

Lysa Wren's activism emphasizes the importance of challenging the norms associated with femininity. This includes questioning the societal pressure to conform to traditional standards of beauty, behavior, and roles. For example, the expectation that women should prioritize nurturing and caregiving can be limiting and excludes those who may not fit into these roles, such as women who choose to pursue careers or those who identify as non-binary or genderqueer.

Moreover, the fetishization of femininity in media and advertising often perpetuates harmful stereotypes. The portrayal of women as passive, delicate, and dependent reinforces a narrow view of femininity that many activists, including Wren, seek to dismantle. By advocating for a broader representation of femininity that includes strength, assertiveness, and independence, Wren aims to empower individuals to embrace their authentic selves.

Intersectionality and Femininity

It is crucial to recognize that femininity is experienced differently across various intersecting identities, including race, class, sexuality, and ability. The concept of intersectionality, coined by Kimberlé Crenshaw, underscores that the experiences of women cannot be generalized; rather, they are shaped by the interplay of multiple social identities. For instance, a Black woman may face unique challenges that differ from those of a white woman, particularly regarding societal expectations of femininity.

Wren's advocacy includes amplifying the voices of marginalized groups within the feminist movement. She emphasizes that true deconstruction of femininity must involve an understanding of how race, class, and sexuality intersect to create diverse experiences of womanhood. This approach fosters inclusivity and ensures that the movement does not erase the realities faced by women of color, LGBTQ+ individuals, and those from lower socioeconomic backgrounds.

Examples of Deconstructing Femininity

One prominent example of deconstructing femininity can be seen in the rise of body positivity movements that challenge conventional beauty standards. Activists like Ashley Graham and Lizzo promote self-love and acceptance, encouraging individuals to embrace their bodies regardless of societal expectations. This movement aligns with Wren's vision of redefining femininity to include a broader range of body types, styles, and self-expressions.

Furthermore, the emergence of gender-neutral fashion is another facet of this deconstruction. Designers such as Telfar Clemens and brands like A.P.C. challenge traditional gendered clothing by creating collections that are accessible to all genders. This shift not only allows individuals to express themselves beyond the confines of femininity and masculinity but also promotes a more inclusive understanding of gender.

Conclusion

Deconstructing femininity is a vital aspect of Lysa Wren's activism, as it encourages individuals to question societal norms and embrace their identities authentically. By challenging the traditional constructs of femininity, Wren advocates for a more inclusive and diverse representation of womanhood that recognizes the complexity of gender. This deconstruction fosters empowerment, self-acceptance, and solidarity among individuals across various identities, ultimately contributing to a more equitable society.

In the words of Wren, "To be truly free, we must dismantle the cages built by society and redefine what it means to be feminine on our own terms."

Embracing Fluidity and Non-Binary Identities

In recent years, the conversation surrounding gender has evolved significantly, moving beyond the rigid binary constructs of male and female. Embracing fluidity and non-binary identities is an essential aspect of Lysa Wren's activism, which challenges traditional understandings of gender and promotes a more inclusive society.

Understanding Gender Fluidity

Gender fluidity refers to a flexible range of gender identities that may change over time or depending on the context. Unlike the binary model, which categorizes individuals strictly as male or female, gender fluidity acknowledges that gender can be a spectrum. This perspective aligns with Judith Butler's theory of gender performativity, which posits that gender is not an inherent trait but rather a performance shaped by societal norms and expectations.

$$G = P \times S \tag{11}$$

Where G represents gender identity, P signifies personal expression, and S symbolizes societal expectations. This equation illustrates how individual identity is influenced by both personal choices and external societal pressures.

The Non-Binary Experience

Non-binary individuals identify outside the traditional male-female binary. This can encompass a variety of identities, including genderqueer, agender, bigender, and more. According to the 2020 U.S. Transgender Survey, approximately 11% of respondents identified as non-binary, highlighting the growing recognition of these identities.

The challenges faced by non-binary individuals are manifold, ranging from societal misunderstanding to systemic discrimination. Many non-binary people report difficulties in accessing healthcare, legal recognition, and social acceptance. For instance, the lack of non-binary options on legal documents, such as passports and driver's licenses, often forces individuals to choose a binary option that does not reflect their identity.

Language and Representation

Language plays a crucial role in the recognition and validation of non-binary identities. The use of inclusive language, such as they/them pronouns, is vital for fostering an environment where non-binary individuals feel seen and respected. Lysa Wren has been a vocal advocate for the adoption of gender-neutral language, arguing that language shapes our understanding of identity.

$$L = I + R \tag{12}$$

Where L represents language, I symbolizes identity, and R denotes representation. This equation suggests that the way we speak about gender influences how identities are perceived and validated within society.

Intersectionality and Non-Binary Identities

It is essential to consider the intersectionality of non-binary identities, as race, class, sexuality, and other factors intersect to shape individual experiences. Non-binary individuals from marginalized communities often face compounded discrimination. For instance, a non-binary person of color may encounter racism alongside gender discrimination, creating unique challenges that require a nuanced understanding of their identity.

Cultural Perspectives on Non-Binary Identities

Globally, various cultures have recognized non-binary identities long before contemporary discussions. The hijra community in South Asia, Two-Spirit identities among Indigenous peoples in North America, and fa'afafine in Samoa are examples of gender non-conformity that have existed for centuries. These cultural frameworks challenge Western notions of gender and highlight the need for a more inclusive understanding of identity.

Promoting Acceptance and Understanding

To embrace fluidity and non-binary identities, society must work towards greater acceptance and understanding. Education plays a pivotal role in this process, as it can dispel myths and misconceptions surrounding non-binary identities. Lysa Wren has actively engaged in educational initiatives, emphasizing the importance of workshops and community dialogues to foster empathy and understanding.

Conclusion

Embracing fluidity and non-binary identities is a crucial aspect of Lysa Wren's activism, as it challenges traditional gender norms and promotes inclusivity. By understanding the complexities of gender, advocating for inclusive language, and recognizing the intersectionality of identities, society can move towards a more equitable future. The journey towards acceptance is ongoing, but through awareness and education, individuals can cultivate a culture that honors diversity and authenticity.

The Importance of Intersectionality

Intersectionality is a critical framework that explores how various social identities—such as race, gender, sexuality, class, and ability—interact and contribute to unique experiences of oppression and privilege. Coined by Kimberlé Crenshaw in 1989, intersectionality challenges the idea that social categories exist in isolation. Instead, it posits that individuals experience overlapping and interdependent systems of discrimination or disadvantage. In the context of LGBTQ activism, intersectionality is vital for understanding the diverse experiences within the community and advocating for a more inclusive movement.

Theoretical Foundations

At its core, intersectionality recognizes that identities are not singular; they are multifaceted and shaped by various social contexts. For instance, a Black transgender woman experiences discrimination not only based on her gender identity but also through the lens of race and socioeconomic status. This compounded marginalization can lead to unique challenges that are often overlooked in mainstream LGBTQ activism, which may predominantly focus on issues faced by white, cisgender individuals.

Theoretical frameworks that support intersectionality include:

+ **Social Constructivism:** This theory posits that identities are constructed through social interactions and cultural contexts. It emphasizes that societal norms dictate the perception of gender and sexuality, thus shaping the lived experiences of individuals.

+ **Critical Race Theory:** This framework examines the relationship between race, law, and power. It highlights how systemic racism intersects with other forms of discrimination, impacting marginalized groups within the LGBTQ community.

+ **Queer Theory:** This perspective challenges the binary understanding of gender and sexuality, advocating for a more fluid interpretation of identity. It aligns with intersectionality by recognizing that individuals cannot be defined solely by one aspect of their identity.

Real-World Implications

Understanding intersectionality is crucial for addressing the specific needs of marginalized groups within the LGBTQ community. For example, LGBTQ individuals of color often face higher rates of violence, discrimination, and economic instability compared to their white counterparts. According to the Human Rights Campaign, Black LGBTQ individuals are more likely to experience homelessness and unemployment due to the intersection of race and sexual orientation.

Moreover, the intersection of gender identity and socioeconomic status can lead to significant disparities in access to healthcare. Transgender individuals, particularly those from low-income backgrounds, may encounter barriers to receiving necessary medical treatments, such as hormone therapy or gender-affirming surgeries. These barriers are exacerbated for individuals who also belong to racial minorities, highlighting the need for an intersectional approach in advocacy efforts.

Examples of Intersectional Activism

Lysa Wren's activism exemplifies the importance of intersectionality in LGBTQ movements. By amplifying the voices of individuals from diverse backgrounds, she has highlighted the unique challenges faced by various groups. For instance, her collaboration with organizations focused on racial justice has brought attention to the experiences of LGBTQ people of color, advocating for policies that address both racial and LGBTQ discrimination.

An illustrative case is the #BlackTransLivesMatter movement, which emerged as a response to the violence disproportionately affecting Black transgender individuals. This movement emphasizes the intersection of race and gender identity, advocating for justice and equality for those who are often marginalized within both racial and LGBTQ communities. By focusing on intersectionality, activists can create more comprehensive strategies that address the root causes of oppression.

Challenges and Critiques

While intersectionality is a powerful tool for understanding and addressing inequalities, it is not without its challenges. One significant issue is the potential for fragmentation within the LGBTQ movement. As various groups advocate for their specific needs, there is a risk of diluting the overall message of equality and inclusion. Activists must navigate the delicate balance between highlighting individual experiences and fostering solidarity among diverse identities.

Additionally, there is a critique that intersectionality can sometimes lead to a hierarchy of oppression, where certain identities are prioritized over others. This can create tension among activists and hinder collaboration. It is essential for movements to embrace a holistic approach that recognizes the interconnectedness of various struggles without diminishing the importance of any single issue.

Conclusion

In conclusion, the importance of intersectionality in LGBTQ activism cannot be overstated. By acknowledging the complex interplay of identities, activists can develop more inclusive and effective strategies that address the unique challenges faced by marginalized groups. Lysa Wren's work serves as a testament to the power of intersectional advocacy, inspiring others to embrace diversity and champion the rights of all individuals, regardless of their intersecting identities. As the fight for equality continues, understanding and implementing intersectionality will be crucial in creating a more just and equitable society for everyone.

A Call for Inclusive Language

Language is a powerful tool that shapes our perceptions of identity and society. In the realm of LGBTQ activism, inclusive language serves as a cornerstone for fostering understanding and acceptance. Lysa Wren understands that words carry weight; they can uplift or marginalize, empower or diminish. This section delves into the significance of inclusive language, the challenges associated with it, and practical examples of its implementation.

Theoretical Underpinnings

Inclusive language is rooted in the theory of linguistic relativity, which posits that the structure of a language affects its speakers' worldview. As noted by [?], the way we articulate our thoughts influences our perceptions of reality. Thus, using inclusive language can help dismantle harmful stereotypes and promote a more equitable society.

$$\text{Inclusive Language} = \text{Language that acknowledges diversity and promotes equality} \tag{13}$$

This equation highlights that inclusive language is not merely about avoiding offensive terms; it is about actively recognizing and celebrating diversity. Lysa emphasizes that language should reflect the complexities of gender and sexuality, rather than confining individuals to outdated binary categories.

Problems with Exclusive Language

Exclusive language perpetuates stereotypes and reinforces societal norms that marginalize individuals. For example, traditional gendered terms such as "mankind" or "chairman" imply a male-centric viewpoint, effectively erasing the contributions of women and non-binary individuals. The use of such language can lead to feelings of alienation among those who do not identify with the dominant group.

Moreover, the failure to use correct pronouns can have profound effects on mental health. Research by [?] indicates that individuals who are misgendered experience increased levels of anxiety and depression. This highlights the urgent need for activists like Lysa Wren to advocate for language that affirms identities and promotes mental well-being.

Practical Examples of Inclusive Language

Lysa Wren's activism includes practical strategies for implementing inclusive language in everyday conversations. Here are some key recommendations:

- **Use Gender-Neutral Terms:** Replace binary terms with gender-neutral alternatives. For example, use "humankind" instead of "mankind" and "chairperson" instead of "chairman."

- **Ask for Pronouns:** Create a culture of respect by asking individuals for their preferred pronouns. This simple act can validate a person's identity and foster an inclusive environment.

- **Avoid Assumptions:** Refrain from making assumptions about someone's gender or sexual orientation based on their appearance. Instead, engage in open dialogue that allows individuals to express their identities on their terms.

- **Use Inclusive Phrases:** Incorporate phrases that acknowledge diverse identities, such as "partner" instead of "husband" or "wife," to encompass all forms of relationships.

Challenges in Implementing Inclusive Language

Despite the clear benefits, the transition to inclusive language is fraught with challenges. Many individuals resist change due to entrenched beliefs and societal conditioning. Lysa Wren encounters backlash when advocating for inclusive terminology, often from those who perceive it as a threat to traditional values.

Additionally, the evolving nature of language can create confusion. Terms that are widely accepted today may become outdated tomorrow, necessitating continuous learning and adaptation. Lysa encourages her followers to embrace this fluidity, reminding them that language is a living entity that reflects societal changes.

Conclusion

Lysa Wren's call for inclusive language is not merely a suggestion; it is a demand for respect and recognition in a world that often marginalizes diverse identities. By advocating for language that acknowledges and celebrates differences, she paves the way for a more inclusive society. The journey toward inclusive language is ongoing, but it is essential for dismantling barriers and fostering understanding among all individuals.

In the words of Lysa, "Language is the bridge we build to connect hearts and minds. Let us ensure that bridge is wide enough for everyone to cross."

Destigmatizing Gender Non-Conformity

The journey towards destigmatizing gender non-conformity is a crucial aspect of Lysa Wren's activism, as it challenges deeply rooted societal norms that dictate how individuals should express their gender. Gender non-conformity refers to behaviors, expressions, and identities that do not align with conventional expectations of masculinity and femininity. This section explores the theoretical frameworks, societal problems, and examples that illustrate the importance of this endeavor.

Theoretical Frameworks

To understand the stigma surrounding gender non-conformity, we can draw on Judith Butler's theory of gender performativity, which posits that gender is not an inherent quality but rather a series of acts and behaviors that society expects individuals to perform. Butler argues that these performances are regulated by societal norms, which can lead to the marginalization of those who do not conform. The equation for understanding gender performance can be expressed as:

$$G = P_1 + P_2 + P_3 + \ldots + P_n \tag{14}$$

where G is gender identity and P_n represents the various performances expected by society. This framework allows us to see how rigid gender norms create a binary system that marginalizes non-conforming identities.

Societal Problems

The stigma attached to gender non-conformity manifests in various societal problems, including discrimination, violence, and mental health issues. According to the Human Rights Campaign, individuals who express gender non-conformity are more likely to experience bullying and harassment in schools and workplaces. The National Center for Transgender Equality reports that nearly 47% of transgender individuals experience sexual assault in their lifetime, a statistic that underscores the urgent need for societal change.

Moreover, the stigmatization of gender non-conformity can lead to internalized homophobia and low self-esteem among individuals who do not fit into traditional gender roles. The psychological impact is profound, as many individuals struggle with their identity in a world that often punishes them for being different.

Examples of Destigmatization Efforts

Lysa Wren's activism is characterized by her efforts to destigmatize gender non-conformity through various initiatives. One notable example is her campaign titled *"Be You, Be Free,"* which encourages individuals to express their true selves without fear of judgment. This campaign utilized social media platforms to share stories of gender non-conforming individuals, creating a sense of community and support.

In addition, Wren collaborated with local schools to implement educational programs that address gender diversity. These programs aim to foster understanding and acceptance among students, providing them with the tools to challenge stereotypes. By integrating discussions about gender non-conformity into school curricula, Wren's initiatives have contributed to a more inclusive environment.

The Role of Media and Representation

Media representation plays a significant role in destigmatizing gender non-conformity. Positive portrayals of gender non-conforming individuals in film, television, and literature can challenge stereotypes and promote acceptance. For instance, the character of *Billy* in the musical *"Billy Elliot"* showcases the journey of a boy who defies traditional gender roles by pursuing ballet. This representation not only highlights the struggles faced by gender non-conforming individuals but also celebrates their resilience.

Moreover, social media influencers who embrace gender fluidity and non-binary identities have become powerful advocates for change. By sharing their experiences and challenging norms, they inspire others to embrace their authentic selves.

Conclusion

Destigmatizing gender non-conformity is essential for creating a society that values diversity and authenticity. Lysa Wren's efforts serve as a beacon of hope for many individuals who feel marginalized due to their gender expression. By challenging societal norms, advocating for education, and promoting positive representation, Wren and her allies are paving the way for a more inclusive future.

The journey is ongoing, but as Wren often reminds us, "*Every step towards acceptance is a step towards freedom.*"

Elevating Transgender Voices

In the landscape of LGBTQ activism, the elevation of transgender voices is not merely an act of inclusion; it is a fundamental necessity for the advancement of equality and justice. Transgender individuals have historically faced marginalization, discrimination, and violence, which necessitates a focused effort to amplify their narratives and experiences. Lysa Wren recognizes this urgency and has made it a cornerstone of her activism, understanding that the visibility of transgender voices can challenge societal norms and foster understanding.

Theoretical Framework

The theoretical underpinnings of elevating transgender voices can be rooted in intersectionality, a concept coined by Kimberlé Crenshaw. Intersectionality posits that individuals experience multiple, overlapping identities that shape their experiences of oppression and privilege. For transgender individuals, these identities can include race, class, sexual orientation, and ability, among others. By recognizing the complexity of these intersections, activists can better advocate for a more inclusive and nuanced understanding of transgender issues.

$$P = \sum_{i=1}^{n}(x_i \cdot w_i) \tag{15}$$

where P represents the overall impact of advocacy efforts, x_i represents the individual experiences of transgender individuals, and w_i represents the weight of each identity factor in shaping those experiences. This equation illustrates that the collective impact of elevating transgender voices is multifaceted and influenced by various identity intersections.

Challenges Faced by Transgender Individuals

Despite the progress made in LGBTQ rights, transgender individuals continue to face significant challenges. According to the Human Rights Campaign, transgender people are disproportionately affected by violence, with 2020 marking one of the deadliest years on record for transgender individuals in the United

States. Additionally, many transgender individuals encounter systemic barriers in healthcare, employment, and housing, which further marginalizes their voices.

$$D = \frac{V_t}{C} \tag{16}$$

where D represents the degree of discrimination faced by transgender individuals, V_t is the number of reported incidents of discrimination, and C is the total population of transgender individuals. This equation highlights the pervasive nature of discrimination within the transgender community, emphasizing the need for advocacy and support.

Strategies for Elevation

Lysa Wren employs several strategies to elevate transgender voices within her activism:

- **Creating Safe Spaces:** Wren organizes community forums and workshops that provide safe spaces for transgender individuals to share their stories and experiences. These platforms allow for authentic dialogue and foster a sense of community.

- **Utilizing Media:** Understanding the power of media, Wren encourages transgender individuals to share their narratives through various channels, including social media, blogs, and podcasts. This not only amplifies their voices but also educates the broader public about transgender issues.

- **Advocating for Representation:** Wren actively campaigns for greater representation of transgender individuals in media, politics, and leadership roles. She believes that visibility in these spheres is crucial for changing perceptions and dismantling stereotypes.

- **Collaborative Efforts:** By building alliances with other LGBTQ organizations and movements, Wren ensures that transgender voices are included in broader discussions about rights and policies. This collaborative approach amplifies the message and creates a unified front for change.

Examples of Impact

One notable example of elevating transgender voices is the case of the Transgender Day of Remembrance (TDOR), an annual observance that honors the lives lost to anti-transgender violence. Lysa Wren has played a pivotal role in organizing local

TDOR events, providing a platform for transgender individuals to share their stories and remember those who have been lost. This observance not only raises awareness about violence against transgender people but also fosters a sense of solidarity within the community.

Moreover, Wren's involvement in the "Proud & Unapologetic" movement has led to the creation of educational programs aimed at schools and workplaces. These programs focus on transgender awareness and inclusivity, providing resources for individuals and institutions to support transgender individuals better. By fostering understanding and empathy, these initiatives contribute to a cultural shift that recognizes and values transgender voices.

Conclusion

Elevating transgender voices is an essential aspect of Lysa Wren's activism and the broader LGBTQ movement. By addressing the unique challenges faced by transgender individuals and employing strategic methods to amplify their narratives, Wren not only advocates for justice but also inspires a generation to embrace diversity and authenticity. The journey toward equality is ongoing, and the elevation of transgender voices remains a vital component in the fight for a more inclusive society.

Promoting Self-Acceptance and Self-Love

In a world that often imposes rigid standards of identity and behavior, Lysa Wren has emerged as a beacon of self-acceptance and self-love, advocating for individuals to embrace their authentic selves without fear or shame. This section explores the theoretical frameworks surrounding self-acceptance, the challenges many face in achieving it, and practical examples of how Lysa's activism has fostered a culture of love and acceptance.

Theoretical Frameworks

Self-acceptance is defined as the recognition and acceptance of one's own feelings, thoughts, and values, as well as the acknowledgment of one's own strengths and weaknesses. According to [?], self-acceptance is a crucial component of self-compassion, which involves treating oneself with kindness in the face of suffering or failure. This perspective is particularly relevant in LGBTQ activism, where individuals often face societal rejection and internalized stigma.

The **Theory of Planned Behavior** (Ajzen, 1991) can also be applied here, suggesting that attitudes towards self-acceptance, subjective norms, and perceived behavioral control influence an individual's intention to engage in self-acceptance practices. For LGBTQ individuals, societal attitudes can significantly impact their self-perception and acceptance.

Challenges to Self-Acceptance

Despite the theoretical frameworks that support self-acceptance, many individuals face significant barriers. Internalized homophobia, defined as the internalization of societal stigma against LGBTQ identities, can lead to self-hatred and denial of one's true self. This phenomenon is often exacerbated by cultural and familial rejection, which can create a pervasive sense of unworthiness.

Moreover, societal pressures to conform to traditional gender norms can lead individuals to suppress their authentic identities. Lysa Wren's advocacy work addresses these issues head-on, promoting the idea that self-acceptance is not only possible but essential for personal and communal growth.

Lysa Wren's Advocacy for Self-Acceptance

Lysa has utilized various platforms to promote self-acceptance and self-love, notably through her writing and public speaking engagements. Her literary works often reflect her journey of self-discovery and acceptance, resonating with those who feel marginalized. For instance, in her poem collection *Unveiling the Soul*, Lysa articulates the struggles of coming to terms with one's identity, using vivid imagery and relatable narratives to connect with her audience.

$$\text{Self-Acceptance} = \text{Authenticity} + \text{Self-Love} + \text{Empathy} \qquad (17)$$

This equation illustrates that self-acceptance arises from a combination of being true to oneself, cultivating self-love, and fostering empathy towards oneself and others. Lysa emphasizes that self-love is not narcissism; rather, it is an acknowledgment of one's worthiness and the importance of nurturing oneself.

Practical Examples of Self-Acceptance Initiatives

In her community, Lysa has spearheaded several initiatives aimed at promoting self-acceptance. One notable example is the "Love Yourself First" workshop series, where participants engage in activities designed to explore their identities and embrace their uniqueness. These workshops incorporate art therapy, storytelling, and group discussions, creating a safe space for individuals to share their experiences and learn from one another.

Additionally, Lysa's social media campaigns, such as the hashtag #ProudAndUnapologetic, have encouraged individuals to share their stories of self-acceptance. This movement has garnered widespread participation, illustrating the power of community in fostering self-love.

The Impact of Self-Acceptance on Mental Health

Research has shown that self-acceptance is linked to improved mental health outcomes. A study by [?] found that individuals who practice self-acceptance report lower levels of anxiety and depression. For LGBTQ individuals, embracing their identities can lead to increased resilience against societal stigma and discrimination.

Lysa Wren's message of self-acceptance is particularly vital in this context. By encouraging individuals to embrace their true selves, she not only fosters personal growth but also contributes to a broader cultural shift towards acceptance and understanding.

Conclusion

Promoting self-acceptance and self-love is a cornerstone of Lysa Wren's activism. Through her advocacy, she challenges societal norms and encourages individuals to embrace their identities fully. By addressing the barriers to self-acceptance and providing practical tools for individuals to cultivate self-love, Lysa's work continues to inspire countless others on their journeys toward authenticity. In a world that often seeks to divide, her message remains clear: love yourself unapologetically, for that is where true empowerment begins.

Navigating Relationships and Intimacy

In the journey of self-discovery and activism, Lysa Wren found that navigating relationships and intimacy presented both challenges and opportunities for growth. As she deconstructed the rigid frameworks of gender norms, she also had to confront the complexities of her own emotional landscape. This section explores the multifaceted nature of relationships within the LGBTQ community, focusing on intimacy, communication, and the importance of authenticity.

The Complexity of Intimacy

Intimacy is often perceived through a heteronormative lens, which can alienate those who identify outside traditional gender binaries. Lysa recognized that intimacy is not solely defined by physical closeness but also encompasses emotional and psychological connections. This understanding aligns with the theories of attachment styles, which suggest that individuals approach intimacy based on their early relational experiences.

$$I = \frac{E + C + P}{N} \tag{18}$$

Where I represents intimacy, E is emotional connection, C is communication, P is physical closeness, and N is the number of partners involved. This equation illustrates that intimacy can be cultivated through various dimensions, emphasizing the importance of emotional and communicative aspects over mere physicality.

Challenges in LGBTQ Relationships

Lysa faced unique challenges in her relationships, often stemming from societal stigma and internalized biases. For example, many LGBTQ individuals experience what is termed "relationship anarchy," which rejects traditional monogamous structures in favor of more fluid arrangements. While this approach can foster freedom and exploration, it can also lead to misunderstandings and emotional turmoil if partners are not on the same page regarding expectations.

In her own relationships, Lysa encountered the struggle of balancing her identity with societal expectations. The fear of rejection often loomed large, impacting her ability to form deep connections. This aligns with the concept of "minority stress," which posits that marginalized individuals experience chronic stress due to their social identities, affecting their relationships and mental health.

Communication as a Tool for Connection

To navigate these complexities, Lysa emphasized the importance of open communication. She believed that discussing boundaries, desires, and fears was crucial for building trust and intimacy. The practice of "radical honesty," where partners commit to sharing their true feelings and thoughts without filters, became a cornerstone of her relationships.

For instance, during her involvement in the "Proud & Unapologetic" movement, Lysa encouraged her partners to engage in regular check-ins, fostering a culture of transparency. This practice not only enhanced emotional intimacy but also allowed her to explore her own evolving identity in relation to her partners.

Exploring Non-Traditional Relationship Models

Lysa's activism also led her to explore various relationship models beyond monogamy. Polyamory, for instance, became a significant aspect of her relational landscape. By embracing multiple romantic connections, she found that love could be expansive rather than finite. This shift in perspective was liberating, as it allowed her to experience intimacy with diverse individuals, each contributing uniquely to her understanding of love and connection.

However, this model also required continuous negotiation and communication. Lysa and her partners often engaged in discussions about jealousy, time management, and emotional support, reinforcing the idea that intimacy is an active, ongoing process rather than a static state.

The Role of Self-Acceptance in Relationships

Crucially, Lysa discovered that self-acceptance played a pivotal role in her ability to form healthy relationships. As she learned to embrace her own identity, she found that vulnerability became a powerful tool for connection. Sharing her insecurities and fears with partners not only deepened their bond but also created a space for mutual growth and understanding.

In her writings, Lysa often referenced the importance of self-love as a precursor to healthy relationships. She posited that one cannot fully engage in intimate connections without first nurturing a loving relationship with oneself. This idea is encapsulated in the following equation:

$$R = S + E \tag{19}$$

Where R represents relationship satisfaction, S is self-love, and E is emotional engagement. This equation underscores the necessity of self-acceptance as a foundation for fulfilling relationships.

Conclusion: The Journey of Intimacy

Navigating relationships and intimacy was an integral part of Lysa Wren's journey as an activist. Through her experiences, she learned that intimacy is not a one-size-fits-all concept but rather a fluid, evolving process that requires ongoing communication, self-acceptance, and an openness to explore non-traditional models. By breaking down gender norms and embracing the complexities of love, Lysa not only transformed her own life but also inspired others to seek authentic connections in their relationships. Her legacy continues to remind us that intimacy, in all its forms, is a vital aspect of the human experience, deserving of celebration and exploration.

Inspiring Empathy and Understanding

In a world often divided by rigid categories and preconceived notions, Lysa Wren emerged as a beacon of empathy and understanding, advocating for a profound shift in how society perceives gender and identity. Her approach was rooted in the belief that genuine connection and compassion are essential for dismantling the barriers that separate individuals from one another. This section explores the theoretical frameworks that underpin Wren's activism, the challenges she faced, and the impactful examples she set forth to inspire empathy and understanding in Velmar and beyond.

Theoretical Frameworks

At the heart of Lysa Wren's activism lies the concept of *empathy*, defined as the capacity to understand and share the feelings of another. According to *Carl Rogers*, a prominent psychologist, empathy is not merely a passive experience; it requires an active engagement with another's emotional state. Wren utilized this theory in her outreach, encouraging individuals to not only listen but to truly *hear* the stories of those who differ from them.

The *Intersectionality Theory*, developed by *Kimberlé Crenshaw*, also played a pivotal role in Wren's advocacy. This framework emphasizes that individuals experience oppression and privilege in varying degrees based on their intersecting identities, such as race, gender, and sexual orientation. By applying this theory, Wren highlighted the importance of understanding how different identities interact, fostering a more nuanced comprehension of the struggles faced by marginalized communities.

Challenges Faced

Despite her commitment to promoting empathy, Wren encountered significant challenges. One of the most pressing issues was the pervasive culture of *misunderstanding* that often leads to prejudice and discrimination. Many individuals in Velmar, influenced by traditional gender norms, struggled to accept non-binary identities and expressions. Wren recognized that these societal attitudes were deeply ingrained, often stemming from fear and ignorance.

Moreover, Wren faced backlash from both conservative factions and even some within the LGBTQ community who were resistant to her inclusive approach. The challenge was not only to promote understanding but also to combat the *internalized biases* that many individuals held, including those who identified as LGBTQ. This internal conflict often manifested as a reluctance to fully embrace the fluidity of gender, leading to a fragmented sense of community.

Examples of Empathy in Action

To combat these challenges, Lysa Wren implemented several initiatives aimed at fostering empathy and understanding. One notable example was her organization of community workshops titled *"Voices of Velmar,"* where individuals from diverse backgrounds shared their personal stories. These gatherings provided a safe space for dialogue, allowing participants to confront their biases and engage with the lived experiences of others.

Wren also initiated a campaign called *"Walk in My Shoes,"* which encouraged people to participate in role-reversal exercises. Participants were invited to experience a day in the life of someone from a different gender identity or sexual orientation. This immersive approach not only fostered empathy but also illuminated the daily challenges faced by marginalized individuals, effectively humanizing abstract concepts.

Furthermore, Wren leveraged social media as a platform for storytelling. By sharing powerful narratives and testimonials from individuals across the gender spectrum, she created a digital space for connection and understanding. The hashtag *"#EmpathyInAction"* gained traction, enabling users to share their own stories and engage with a wider audience, thereby fostering a sense of solidarity and community.

The Ripple Effect of Empathy

The impact of Wren's efforts in inspiring empathy and understanding extended beyond individual interactions; it catalyzed a ripple effect throughout Velmar society. As more individuals engaged with her initiatives, the community began to shift towards a culture of acceptance and inclusivity. Schools implemented programs that emphasized empathy training, encouraging students to explore the complexities of identity and the importance of kindness.

Moreover, local businesses started to adopt inclusive policies, recognizing that fostering an empathetic workplace not only benefited employees but also enhanced overall productivity and morale. Wren's advocacy demonstrated that empathy is not a finite resource; rather, it can be cultivated and expanded, leading to a more compassionate society.

Conclusion

In conclusion, Lysa Wren's commitment to inspiring empathy and understanding has left an indelible mark on Velmar. By employing theoretical frameworks, confronting challenges head-on, and implementing tangible initiatives, she has paved the way for a more inclusive society. Her legacy serves as a reminder that empathy is not merely a passive emotion but an active force that can drive change, foster connection, and ultimately bridge the divides that separate us. As Wren often stated, *"To understand is to be human; to empathize is to be alive."* Through her unyielding dedication, she has shown that the journey towards understanding is one that requires courage, vulnerability, and a commitment to authenticity.

Advocacy and Activism

Fighting for Legal Protections

The Battle for Marriage Equality

The struggle for marriage equality stands as one of the most pivotal battles in the broader LGBTQ rights movement. It encapsulates not only the desire for legal recognition of love but also the fight against deep-seated societal prejudices. This section delves into the theoretical underpinnings, challenges faced, and notable examples that illustrate the significance of marriage equality within the context of Lysa Wren's activism.

Theoretical Framework

At its core, the fight for marriage equality can be analyzed through the lens of several key theories. First, the **Social Contract Theory** posits that individuals consent to form societies and abide by mutual agreements for the benefit of all. In this context, denying same-sex couples the right to marry can be viewed as a violation of this contract, as it denies them the same legal and social recognition afforded to heterosexual couples.

Moreover, **Queer Theory** challenges the conventional norms surrounding sexuality and gender, arguing for the deconstruction of binary classifications. This theory supports the notion that marriage should not be confined to heterosexual unions, but rather should encompass all forms of love and partnership, thereby promoting inclusivity.

Historical Context and Legal Challenges

The battle for marriage equality has a rich history marked by significant legal challenges. In the United States, the landmark case of *Baker v. Nelson* (1971) was one of the first to address the issue, where the Minnesota Supreme Court dismissed a same-sex couple's appeal for a marriage license. This case set a precedent that would linger for decades, reinforcing the notion that marriage was a heteronormative institution.

However, the tide began to shift with the emergence of cases like *Goodridge v. Department of Public Health* (2003), where the Massachusetts Supreme Judicial Court ruled that same-sex couples had the right to marry, marking the first time a U.S. state legalized same-sex marriage. This decision ignited a wave of activism, with Lysa Wren emerging as a prominent voice advocating for similar rights across the nation.

Cultural Resistance and Backlash

Despite progress, the fight for marriage equality was met with significant cultural resistance. Many opponents framed the issue as a threat to traditional family values, often invoking religious beliefs to justify their stance. The passage of constitutional amendments banning same-sex marriage in several states, such as California's Proposition 8 in 2008, illustrated the backlash faced by the LGBTQ community.

Lysa Wren, through her activism, sought to dismantle these arguments by emphasizing the importance of love and commitment. She often quoted Martin Luther King Jr., stating, "Injustice anywhere is a threat to justice everywhere," underscoring the interconnectedness of civil rights struggles.

The Role of Activism and Public Opinion

Activism played a crucial role in shifting public opinion on marriage equality. Organizations such as the Human Rights Campaign and GLAAD mobilized resources to educate the public and advocate for legislative change. Social media emerged as a powerful tool, allowing activists like Lysa to reach wider audiences and foster dialogue.

The **Proud & Unapologetic** movement, founded by Lysa Wren, utilized platforms like Twitter and Instagram to share personal stories and testimonials from same-sex couples, humanizing the issue and fostering empathy. This grassroots approach was instrumental in changing hearts and minds, contributing to a significant shift in public opinion by the early 2010s.

The Supreme Court Decision

The culmination of these efforts came with the historic Supreme Court ruling in *Obergefell v. Hodges* (2015), which legalized same-sex marriage nationwide. The Court's decision rested on the principles of equal protection and due process, affirming that the right to marry is a fundamental liberty inherent to the dignity of individuals.

Lysa Wren celebrated this victory not only as a personal triumph but as a collective achievement for the LGBTQ community. In her speeches, she emphasized that while the ruling was a significant step forward, it was not the end of the struggle. "Marriage equality is a foundation, not a ceiling," she proclaimed, calling for continued advocacy for comprehensive LGBTQ rights.

The Ongoing Struggle

Despite the legalization of same-sex marriage, challenges persist. Many states continue to enact laws that discriminate against LGBTQ individuals in areas such as employment, healthcare, and education. Lysa Wren's activism has evolved to address these ongoing issues, advocating for comprehensive anti-discrimination laws that protect LGBTQ individuals in all aspects of life.

The battle for marriage equality serves as a reminder that the fight for LGBTQ rights is ongoing. Lysa Wren's journey exemplifies the resilience and determination of activists who continue to challenge societal norms and advocate for a world where love knows no bounds.

In conclusion, the fight for marriage equality is a testament to the power of activism, community support, and the relentless pursuit of justice. As Lysa Wren continues to inspire future generations, her legacy will remind us that every battle fought in the name of love brings us one step closer to a more inclusive society.

$$\text{Equality} = \text{Love} + \text{Justice} \tag{20}$$

Securing Employment and Housing Rights

In the landscape of LGBTQ activism, securing employment and housing rights is a critical pillar that supports the broader fight for equality. Lysa Wren recognized early in her journey that discrimination in these areas not only affects the individual but also perpetuates systemic inequalities within society. This section explores the theoretical frameworks, challenges faced, and notable examples of advocacy efforts aimed at ensuring these fundamental rights.

Theoretical Frameworks

The fight for employment and housing rights can be understood through various theoretical lenses, including social justice theory and intersectionality. Social justice theory posits that all individuals should have equal access to resources and opportunities, which encompasses the right to work and secure housing without fear of discrimination. Intersectionality, introduced by Kimberlé Crenshaw, emphasizes that individuals experience oppression in varied and intersecting ways based on their identities, including gender, sexuality, race, and class. This theory is particularly relevant in understanding the compounded discrimination faced by marginalized members of the LGBTQ community.

Challenges Faced

The challenges in securing employment and housing rights for LGBTQ individuals are multifaceted. Discrimination in hiring practices, workplace harassment, and unjust termination are pervasive issues that many LGBTQ individuals face. According to a 2020 report by the Human Rights Campaign, nearly 50% of LGBTQ workers reported experiencing discrimination at work due to their sexual orientation or gender identity.

In the realm of housing, LGBTQ individuals often encounter biases from landlords and real estate agents, leading to difficulties in securing stable housing. A 2021 study by the Williams Institute revealed that LGBTQ individuals, particularly transgender individuals, are more likely to experience homelessness than their heterosexual counterparts. These challenges are exacerbated for those who belong to multiple marginalized groups, highlighting the urgent need for comprehensive legal protections.

Legal Protections

In response to these challenges, Lysa Wren and her allies advocated for robust legal protections. The Employment Non-Discrimination Act (ENDA), though not yet passed at the federal level, aims to prohibit employment discrimination based on sexual orientation and gender identity. Wren's activism emphasized the importance of local and state-level protections, leading to the enactment of various non-discrimination ordinances across the United States.

Additionally, the Fair Housing Act, originally passed in 1968, prohibits discrimination based on race, color, national origin, religion, sex, familial status, and disability. However, it does not explicitly include sexual orientation or gender identity. Activists like Wren have pushed for amendments to include these categories, arguing that everyone deserves the right to live freely without fear of discrimination.

Notable Examples of Advocacy

One notable example of successful advocacy for employment rights is the case of Aimee Stephens, a transgender woman who was fired from her job for transitioning. Her case reached the Supreme Court in 2020, where the Court ruled that discrimination based on gender identity is a form of sex discrimination under Title VII of the Civil Rights Act. This landmark decision was a significant victory for LGBTQ rights and set a precedent for future employment discrimination cases.

In the housing sector, organizations like the National LGBTQ Task Force have launched campaigns to raise awareness about housing discrimination. They provide resources for LGBTQ individuals facing discrimination and advocate for policy changes at local, state, and national levels. Wren's involvement in these campaigns highlighted the importance of community support and coalition-building in the fight for housing rights.

The Role of Education and Awareness

Education plays a crucial role in combating discrimination in employment and housing. Wren emphasized the importance of training programs for employers and landlords to foster an inclusive environment. Workshops and seminars focused on LGBTQ issues can help dismantle stereotypes and reduce biases, ultimately leading to a more equitable society.

Furthermore, raising awareness about the legal rights of LGBTQ individuals is essential. Many individuals are unaware of their rights and may not report discrimination due to fear of retaliation or lack of knowledge. Wren's efforts included creating informational resources that empower LGBTQ individuals to advocate for themselves and seek legal recourse when necessary.

Conclusion

Securing employment and housing rights remains a vital aspect of the LGBTQ rights movement. Through the lens of social justice and intersectionality, Lysa Wren's advocacy highlights the systemic barriers faced by LGBTQ individuals in these areas. By challenging discriminatory practices, pushing for legal protections, and fostering education and awareness, Wren and her allies work tirelessly to create a more inclusive society where everyone can thrive without fear of discrimination.

The ongoing struggle for these rights is a testament to the resilience of the LGBTQ community and the importance of solidarity in the fight for equality.

$$P(\text{Discrimination}) = P(\text{Employment}) + P(\text{Housing}) + P(\text{Intersectionality}) \tag{21}$$

Where $P(\text{Discrimination})$ represents the likelihood of experiencing discrimination, and each term on the right represents the individual probabilities associated with employment, housing, and the effects of intersecting identities.

Challenging Discrimination in Healthcare

In the journey of LGBTQ activism, one of the most pressing issues that Lysa Wren confronted was the pervasive discrimination within the healthcare system. This systemic bias not only affects access to care but also influences the quality of treatment received by LGBTQ individuals. The healthcare landscape is often marred by a lack of understanding, cultural competency, and sensitivity towards diverse sexual orientations and gender identities. Lysa's advocacy aimed to dismantle these barriers, advocating for policies that promote equitable healthcare access for all.

Understanding Healthcare Discrimination

Healthcare discrimination against LGBTQ individuals can manifest in various forms, including denial of care, inadequate treatment, and refusal to acknowledge patients' identities. Research indicates that many LGBTQ individuals experience discrimination in clinical settings, which can lead to delayed medical treatment and increased health risks. According to the *National LGBTQ Task Force*, approximately 30% of LGBTQ individuals report having experienced discrimination in healthcare settings. Such statistics underscore the urgent need for reform.

Theoretical Framework

To address these issues, Lysa drew upon the *Social Model of Health*, which emphasizes the impact of social factors on health outcomes. This model posits that health disparities are often rooted in societal structures rather than individual behaviors. By applying this framework, Lysa highlighted how systemic inequities, such as economic instability and social stigma, contribute to poorer health outcomes for LGBTQ populations.

Legal and Policy Challenges

Lysa's activism also focused on legal challenges that perpetuate healthcare discrimination. For instance, the lack of comprehensive non-discrimination laws in many regions allows healthcare providers to refuse treatment based on sexual orientation or gender identity. Lysa campaigned for the implementation of policies that protect LGBTQ individuals from discrimination in healthcare, advocating for the inclusion of sexual orientation and gender identity in anti-discrimination laws.

Case Studies

One poignant example of the challenges faced by LGBTQ individuals in healthcare is the case of a transgender woman who was denied hormone therapy by her healthcare provider. This denial not only exacerbated her mental health struggles but also highlighted the need for healthcare professionals to be trained in providing gender-affirming care. Lysa used this case to illustrate the real-world implications of discrimination and the importance of advocating for inclusive healthcare practices.

In another instance, a survey conducted by the *American Medical Association* found that LGBTQ individuals are more likely to avoid seeking medical care due to fear of discrimination. Lysa leveraged these findings to push for training programs aimed at healthcare providers, emphasizing the importance of cultural competency in delivering care to LGBTQ patients.

Advocacy and Activism

Lysa's activism extended beyond raising awareness; she actively participated in organizing workshops and training sessions for healthcare providers. These initiatives aimed to educate professionals about LGBTQ health issues, promote inclusive practices, and foster an environment where patients feel safe and respected. By collaborating with local health organizations, Lysa worked to create resources that would empower LGBTQ individuals to advocate for their own healthcare needs.

Moreover, Lysa utilized social media platforms to amplify her message, sharing personal stories and testimonials from individuals who had faced discrimination in healthcare. This grassroots approach not only humanized the statistics but also fostered a sense of community among those affected.

The Role of Intersectionality

Lysa recognized that healthcare discrimination does not occur in a vacuum; it intersects with various other forms of discrimination, including racism, sexism, and socioeconomic status. By advocating for an intersectional approach to healthcare, Lysa aimed to ensure that the unique challenges faced by LGBTQ individuals of color, low-income individuals, and other marginalized groups were addressed. This approach aligns with the principles of *Intersectionality Theory*, which posits that various social identities intersect to create unique experiences of oppression and privilege.

Conclusion

Through her relentless advocacy, Lysa Wren has made significant strides in challenging healthcare discrimination. By raising awareness, pushing for policy changes, and advocating for cultural competency in healthcare, she has not only impacted the lives of LGBTQ individuals in Velmar but also set a precedent for activism on a global scale. The journey towards equitable healthcare for all is ongoing, but Lysa's contributions serve as a beacon of hope and a call to action for future generations of activists.

Access to Education and Resources

Access to education and resources is a cornerstone of Lysa Wren's advocacy, as she recognized early on that knowledge is power. Education serves not only as a means of personal growth but also as a tool for societal change. In Velmar, where traditional gender norms often dictate the educational landscape, Lysa sought to dismantle barriers that hindered LGBTQ individuals from accessing quality education and resources.

The Educational Gap

The educational gap for LGBTQ individuals is a pressing issue, often exacerbated by systemic discrimination and societal stigma. According to the *National LGBTQ Task Force*, LGBTQ youth are more likely to experience bullying, harassment, and discrimination in educational settings, leading to higher dropout rates and lower academic achievement. This reality is reflected in statistics that show a significant disparity in educational attainment between LGBTQ individuals and their heterosexual counterparts.

$$E = \frac{A}{B} \tag{22}$$

Where:

* E = Educational attainment level

* A = Number of LGBTQ individuals who complete higher education

* B = Total number of LGBTQ individuals

This equation illustrates the ratio of educational success among LGBTQ individuals, highlighting the need for targeted interventions.

Barriers to Access

Lysa identified several barriers to access that LGBTQ individuals face in educational institutions:

* **Discrimination and Bullying:** Many LGBTQ students report feeling unsafe in their schools, leading to absenteeism and disengagement from the educational process.

* **Lack of Inclusive Curriculum:** Traditional curricula often exclude LGBTQ history and contributions, leaving students without representation and context for their identities.

* **Limited Resources:** Many schools lack access to LGBTQ-specific resources, such as counseling services and support groups, which can be crucial for the mental health and well-being of students.

* **Financial Barriers:** Economic disparities can limit access to higher education, with LGBTQ individuals often facing higher rates of poverty and unemployment.

Lysa Wren's Initiatives

In response to these challenges, Lysa Wren launched several initiatives aimed at improving access to education and resources for LGBTQ individuals in Velmar:

- **Scholarship Programs:** Lysa established scholarship funds specifically for LGBTQ students, providing financial assistance to those pursuing higher education. These scholarships not only alleviate financial burdens but also serve as a recognition of the unique challenges faced by these individuals.

- **Inclusive Training for Educators:** Understanding the importance of a supportive educational environment, Lysa advocated for training programs that educate teachers and staff on LGBTQ issues, fostering an inclusive atmosphere for all students.

- **Resource Centers:** Lysa worked to establish LGBTQ resource centers within schools and communities, providing access to information, counseling, and support networks for students and their families.

- **Community Partnerships:** Collaborating with local organizations, Lysa created mentorship programs that connect LGBTQ youth with role models who can provide guidance, support, and encouragement in their educational journeys.

Success Stories

The impact of Lysa's initiatives can be seen in numerous success stories emerging from Velmar. For instance, a local high school student named Jamie, who once struggled with bullying and isolation, found solace in the LGBTQ resource center established by Lysa's advocacy. With access to mentorship and supportive counseling, Jamie not only graduated but also went on to pursue a degree in social work, aiming to give back to the community that supported her.

Another example is the establishment of the *Proud Scholars Program*, which has provided over 100 scholarships to LGBTQ students in Velmar. This program has significantly improved graduation rates among participants, showcasing the transformative power of education when barriers are removed.

Theoretical Framework

Lysa's approach to education access can be framed within the context of *Critical Pedagogy*, which emphasizes the role of education in challenging societal norms and empowering marginalized groups. As theorist Paulo Freire posits, education should be a practice of freedom, enabling individuals to critically engage with their realities and advocate for change.

Furthermore, the principles of *Intersectionality*, as articulated by Kimberlé Crenshaw, underscore the necessity of recognizing how various identities (race, gender, sexuality) intersect to create unique experiences of oppression. Lysa's advocacy for inclusive education reflects this understanding, ensuring that all voices are heard and valued within the educational framework.

Conclusion

Lysa Wren's relentless pursuit of equitable access to education and resources has not only transformed the lives of many individuals in Velmar but has also set a precedent for other communities to follow. By addressing systemic barriers and advocating for inclusive practices, Lysa has created a ripple effect of change that empowers LGBTQ individuals to embrace their identities and pursue their educational aspirations. The journey towards equitable education continues, but Lysa's legacy serves as a beacon of hope and inspiration for future generations.

Promoting LGBTQ-Inclusive Policies

In the landscape of advocacy, promoting LGBTQ-inclusive policies stands as a cornerstone of Lysa Wren's activism. This section delves into the theoretical frameworks, the challenges faced, and the practical examples that illustrate the necessity of such policies in fostering an equitable society.

Theoretical Frameworks

At the heart of LGBTQ-inclusive policy promotion lies the concept of *intersectionality*, a term coined by Kimberlé Crenshaw. Intersectionality posits that individuals experience overlapping social identities, which can lead to unique experiences of discrimination and privilege. For instance, a Black transgender woman may face distinct challenges that differ from those encountered by a white gay man. Understanding these nuances is essential for crafting effective policies that address the needs of all members of the LGBTQ community.

Furthermore, the *Social Model of Disability* can be applied to LGBTQ rights, emphasizing that societal barriers, rather than individual impairments, contribute to discrimination. This model encourages activists to focus on dismantling systemic obstacles that prevent LGBTQ individuals from achieving equality.

Identifying Problems

Despite the progress made in recent years, significant gaps persist in LGBTQ-inclusive policies. Key issues include:

+ **Employment Discrimination:** Many LGBTQ individuals face discrimination in hiring, promotions, and workplace environments. According to a survey by the Human Rights Campaign, nearly 50% of LGBTQ workers reported experiencing discrimination at work.

+ **Healthcare Access:** Disparities in healthcare access and treatment for LGBTQ individuals, particularly transgender people, can lead to poorer health outcomes. A study published in the *American Journal of Public Health* indicated that transgender individuals are more likely to experience barriers to healthcare, including outright refusal of care.

+ **Housing Inequality:** LGBTQ individuals, especially youth, face higher rates of homelessness. The Williams Institute reports that LGBTQ youth are 120% more likely to experience homelessness than their heterosexual peers.

Crafting Inclusive Policies

To address these issues, Lysa Wren and her allies have advocated for comprehensive policies that include:

+ **Non-Discrimination Laws:** Implementing laws that protect individuals from discrimination based on sexual orientation and gender identity in employment, housing, and public accommodations.

+ **Healthcare Reform:** Advocating for policies that ensure equitable access to healthcare for LGBTQ individuals, including gender-affirming treatments and mental health services.

+ **Youth Support Programs:** Establishing programs aimed at supporting LGBTQ youth, particularly those experiencing homelessness or familial rejection.

Real-World Examples

Several successful initiatives illustrate the potential of LGBTQ-inclusive policies:

+ **The Equality Act (USA):** This proposed legislation aims to amend the Civil Rights Act to prohibit discrimination based on sexual orientation and gender identity. While still pending, its introduction has sparked nationwide conversations about the need for comprehensive protections.

- **Transgender Rights in Canada:** The Canadian government has implemented policies to provide healthcare coverage for gender-affirming surgeries, setting a precedent for other nations.

- **Inclusive Education Policies in California:** California's educational policies mandate the inclusion of LGBTQ history and contributions in school curricula, fostering a more inclusive environment for students.

Challenges and Resistance

Despite these advancements, promoting LGBTQ-inclusive policies often encounters resistance. Common challenges include:

- **Political Opposition:** Some lawmakers and advocacy groups oppose LGBTQ rights, framing their arguments around religious freedom or traditional values.

- **Public Misunderstanding:** Misinformation about LGBTQ issues can lead to public resistance against inclusive policies, necessitating robust educational campaigns.

Conclusion

Promoting LGBTQ-inclusive policies is not merely an act of advocacy; it is a fundamental step toward achieving equality and justice for all individuals, regardless of their sexual orientation or gender identity. Lysa Wren's commitment to this cause exemplifies the power of grassroots activism in shaping a more inclusive society. Through intersectional approaches and the dismantling of systemic barriers, the pursuit of LGBTQ rights continues to evolve, inspiring future generations to carry the torch of equality forward.

$$\text{Inclusion} = \frac{\text{Rights} + \text{Access} + \text{Representation}}{\text{Discrimination} + \text{Barriers}} \tag{23}$$

Taking the Fight to the Streets

In the vibrant landscape of LGBTQ activism, few actions resonate as powerfully as the act of taking to the streets. For Lysa Wren, this was not merely a strategic choice; it was a fundamental expression of her identity and a crucial aspect of her advocacy. The streets became her canvas, where she painted the realities of marginalized voices and amplified the call for justice.

Theoretical Framework

To understand the significance of street activism, we can draw from the theory of *social movement mobilization*. According to Tilly and Tarrow (2015), social movements thrive on the collective action of individuals who share common grievances. In Lysa's case, her activism was rooted in the lived experiences of those who faced systemic oppression due to their gender identity and sexual orientation. The streets served as a space for collective expression, where grievances could be voiced and solidarity could be forged.

Identifying Problems

Despite the importance of street activism, Lysa faced numerous challenges. One significant issue was the risk of backlash from conservative factions within Velmar. As protests grew larger, so did the opposition. Activists often found themselves confronting not just ideological differences, but also physical threats. The intersection of activism and public safety raised questions about the efficacy of protest tactics. Lysa had to navigate these treacherous waters, balancing the urgency of her message with the need for safety.

Examples of Activism

Lysa's first major protest was organized in response to a local ordinance that sought to limit the rights of transgender individuals in public spaces. With the slogan *"Trans Rights Are Human Rights"*, she mobilized a diverse coalition of supporters, including allies from various social justice movements. The turnout exceeded expectations, with hundreds taking to the streets, brandishing signs and chanting slogans. This event not only raised awareness but also galvanized local media coverage, bringing attention to the issue at a national level.

$$\text{Protest Impact} = \text{Media Coverage} \times \text{Public Engagement}$$

This equation illustrates how the impact of a protest can be amplified through media coverage and public engagement. Lysa understood that visibility was crucial; thus, she utilized social media platforms to share live updates, photos, and personal stories from the protest. This approach not only informed those unable to attend but also helped build a sense of community among supporters.

Building Alliances

One of the most effective strategies Lysa employed was building alliances with other movements. She recognized that the fight for LGBTQ rights was interconnected with various social justice causes, including racial equality and women's rights. By collaborating with organizations such as the Black Lives Matter movement and local women's shelters, Lysa expanded the reach of her activism. This intersectional approach not only strengthened the message but also fostered a sense of unity among disparate groups.

The Role of Art and Expression

Art played a pivotal role in Lysa's street activism. She believed that creativity could be a powerful tool for social change. During protests, she encouraged participants to express themselves through art, whether it was through painted signs, spoken word poetry, or performances. This artistic expression transformed the streets into a vibrant space of resistance and hope.

$$\text{Artistic Expression} = \text{Creativity} + \text{Activism}$$

This equation highlights how the fusion of creativity and activism can lead to profound social impact. Lysa's use of art not only drew attention to the issues at hand but also allowed participants to process their emotions and experiences in a supportive environment.

Facing Opposition

Despite the successes, Lysa's activism was not without its challenges. She often faced hostility from counter-protesters who vehemently opposed her message. This opposition raised important questions about the role of dissent in a democratic society. Lysa maintained that dissent is a critical component of democracy, arguing that it is through the clash of ideas that progress is made.

$$\text{Progress} = \text{Dialogue} + \text{Dissent}$$

This equation encapsulates Lysa's belief that meaningful dialogue, even in the face of dissent, is essential for societal progress. She encouraged her supporters to engage with opposing viewpoints, not to convert them, but to foster understanding and empathy.

Conclusion

Taking the fight to the streets was a defining aspect of Lysa Wren's activism. Through protests, alliances, and artistic expression, she created a powerful movement that resonated not only in Velmar but beyond. Her ability to navigate challenges, engage with dissent, and amplify marginalized voices solidified her role as a fearless advocate for LGBTQ rights. As she often said, *"The streets belong to those who dare to dream of a better world."* In doing so, she inspired countless others to join the fight, reminding us all that activism is a journey best taken together.

Organizing Protests and Rallies

In the vibrant tapestry of LGBTQ activism, organizing protests and rallies emerges as a powerful tool for change. Lysa Wren, with her indomitable spirit and strategic mind, recognized the importance of these events not just as expressions of dissent but as vital platforms for community solidarity and visibility. This section explores the theory behind organizing protests, the challenges faced, and the impactful examples that shaped Lysa's journey.

Theoretical Framework

At the heart of effective protest organization lies the theory of collective action. According to [?], collective action occurs when individuals come together to pursue a common goal, often in opposition to perceived injustices. Lysa understood that protests serve multiple purposes: they raise awareness, galvanize support, and create a sense of urgency around issues affecting the LGBTQ community.

$$A = f(P, C, T) \tag{24}$$

Where A represents the level of activism, P stands for public perception, C denotes community cohesion, and T signifies the timing of the event. This equation illustrates that successful activism is a function of these interrelated variables.

Challenges in Organizing

Despite the clear benefits, organizing protests is fraught with challenges. Lysa faced significant hurdles, including:

- **Resource Allocation:** Securing funding and resources for materials, permits, and logistics can be daunting. Lysa often turned to crowdfunding and community donations to support her initiatives.

+ **Safety Concerns:** The threat of violence against LGBTQ individuals at protests necessitated careful planning. Lysa collaborated with local law enforcement and community organizations to ensure safety measures were in place.

+ **Diverse Voices:** Ensuring representation from various identities within the LGBTQ spectrum was crucial. Lysa emphasized the importance of intersectionality, as highlighted by [?], to ensure that all voices were heard and valued.

Examples of Impactful Protests

Lysa's activism was marked by several notable protests that left an indelible mark on Velmar's social landscape.

1. **The "Proud & Unapologetic" March** This rally, held annually, was a celebration of LGBTQ pride and a call for equality. Lysa spearheaded the event, which attracted thousands. The march featured speakers from diverse backgrounds, emphasizing the importance of solidarity and collective empowerment. The slogan, "Our Love, Our Voice," resonated deeply, uniting participants under a shared banner of pride.

2. **The "Silence = Death" Vigil** In response to rising violence against LGBTQ individuals, Lysa organized a vigil that transformed into a powerful protest. Participants held candles and wore shirts emblazoned with the phrase "Silence = Death." This event not only honored victims but also demanded action from local leaders. The emotional weight of the vigil captured media attention, amplifying Lysa's message and leading to significant discussions about safety and policy reform.

3. **The "Trans Rights Are Human Rights" Rally** Recognizing the unique challenges faced by the transgender community, Lysa organized this rally to advocate for trans rights. The event included educational workshops, art displays, and personal testimonies that highlighted the struggles and triumphs of transgender individuals. This rally not only raised awareness but also fostered a sense of community and belonging, as participants shared their stories and experiences.

The Power of Social Media

In the digital age, social media has transformed the landscape of protest organization. Lysa adeptly utilized platforms like Twitter and Instagram to mobilize support, disseminate information, and create a sense of urgency. The hashtag #ProudAndUnapologetic trended during her events, showcasing the power of online communities in amplifying grassroots movements.

Conclusion

Organizing protests and rallies is a multifaceted endeavor that requires strategic planning, community engagement, and a deep understanding of the issues at hand. Lysa Wren's efforts in this arena exemplify the transformative power of collective action. Through her unwavering commitment to inclusivity and visibility, Lysa not only challenged the status quo but also inspired countless individuals to join the fight for equality. As she often stated, "When we stand together, our voices become a symphony of change."

Building Alliances with Other Movements

Lysa Wren understood early on that the fight for LGBTQ rights could not exist in a vacuum. To truly dismantle systemic oppression, it was essential to build alliances with other social movements. This strategic approach not only broadened the scope of activism but also reinforced the idea that struggles for justice are interconnected.

Theoretical Framework

The concept of *intersectionality*, coined by Kimberlé Crenshaw, serves as a foundational theory for understanding how different forms of discrimination overlap. Wren's activism exemplified this principle, as she recognized that gender identity, race, class, and sexuality are interwoven aspects of individual identity that impact one's experience of oppression. As Wren often stated, "Our liberation is bound together; when one of us rises, we all rise."

Identifying Common Goals

One of the first steps in building alliances was identifying common goals with other movements. For example, Wren collaborated with feminist organizations to address issues such as domestic violence, which disproportionately affects LGBTQ individuals. By aligning with feminist activists, Wren was able to advocate for comprehensive policies that included protections for all women, regardless of their sexual orientation or gender identity.

Challenges in Alliance Building

Despite the benefits, building alliances was not without its challenges. Wren encountered resistance from some factions within both the LGBTQ community and other movements, where agendas occasionally clashed. For instance, some traditional feminist groups resisted the inclusion of transgender rights, arguing that they diluted the focus on cisgender women's issues. Wren navigated these tensions by facilitating dialogue and emphasizing the importance of a unified front against patriarchy and misogyny.

Examples of Successful Collaborations

A notable example of Wren's successful alliance-building was her partnership with racial justice movements. Understanding that LGBTQ people of color face unique challenges, she worked closely with groups like Black Lives Matter (BLM). This collaboration manifested in joint protests and campaigns that highlighted police violence against marginalized communities. Wren's slogan, "No Justice, No Pride," became a rallying cry that resonated across movements, emphasizing that the fight for LGBTQ rights must include the fight against racial injustice.

Moreover, Wren extended her reach to environmental justice movements, recognizing that climate change disproportionately affects low-income and marginalized communities. By participating in climate strikes and advocating for sustainable policies, she illustrated how environmental degradation intersects with social justice, thereby broadening the narrative of LGBTQ activism.

Creating Safe Spaces for Dialogue

Wren was also instrumental in creating safe spaces for dialogue between different movements. She organized workshops and panels that brought together activists from various backgrounds to share their experiences and strategies. These events often led to the development of collaborative campaigns that addressed multiple forms of oppression, such as the "Queer and Climate Justice" initiative, which aimed to highlight the impact of climate change on LGBTQ communities.

Evaluating Impact and Future Directions

The impact of Wren's alliance-building efforts is evident in the growing recognition of intersectionality within social justice movements. As a result of her work, many organizations have begun to adopt more inclusive practices and policies. However, Wren also acknowledged that the journey is ongoing. She often emphasized the need for continuous evaluation and adaptation of strategies to ensure that all voices are heard and represented.

In conclusion, Lysa Wren's commitment to building alliances with other movements not only strengthened the LGBTQ rights movement but also contributed to a more comprehensive approach to social justice. By recognizing the interconnectedness of various struggles, Wren paved the way for a more inclusive and effective activism that continues to inspire future generations.

The Global Reach of Lysa Wren's Activism

Lysa Wren's activism transcended the borders of Velmar, resonating with individuals and communities around the globe. Her unique approach to LGBTQ rights, particularly her focus on gender fluidity and non-binary identities, became a beacon of hope and inspiration for many who felt marginalized by traditional narratives. This section delves into the expansive influence of Wren's work, exploring how her message of authenticity and inclusivity has sparked movements worldwide.

International Collaborations

One of the cornerstones of Lysa Wren's activism was her commitment to fostering international collaborations. She recognized that the struggles faced by LGBTQ individuals were not confined to Velmar but were a global issue. By partnering with organizations such as *OutRight Action International* and *ILGA World*, Wren helped amplify the voices of activists in countries where LGBTQ rights were severely restricted.

For example, during a pivotal conference in Amsterdam, Wren delivered a speech that highlighted the plight of LGBTQ individuals in countries like Uganda and Chechnya, where anti-LGBTQ laws led to violence and persecution. Her ability to connect the local struggles to a broader global context inspired attendees to take action, resulting in a coalition that advocated for policy changes and increased awareness.

Digital Activism and Social Media

Wren's savvy use of social media platforms played a crucial role in extending her reach. Utilizing platforms such as Twitter, Instagram, and TikTok, she created a digital space where individuals could share their stories, engage in dialogue, and mobilize for change. Her hashtag campaigns, such as #ProudAndUnapologetic, encouraged people from diverse backgrounds to express their identities and challenge societal norms.

The impact of this digital activism was profound. For instance, a viral video of Wren discussing the importance of inclusive language garnered millions of views, sparking conversations in classrooms and workplaces across the globe. This phenomenon illustrated how a single voice could catalyze a worldwide movement, demonstrating the power of social media as a tool for advocacy.

Global Challenges and Responses

Despite the positive strides made through Wren's activism, numerous challenges persist on the global stage. In many countries, LGBTQ individuals face systemic discrimination, violence, and legal barriers. Wren's activism brought attention to these issues, but it also highlighted the need for a multifaceted approach to advocacy.

One pressing issue is the disparity in legal protections for LGBTQ individuals. In regions like the Middle East and parts of Africa, homosexuality is criminalized, leading to severe penalties. Wren's response involved not only raising awareness but also collaborating with local activists to develop strategies for safe advocacy. By providing training and resources, she empowered grassroots movements to challenge oppressive laws while prioritizing the safety of activists on the ground.

Educational Initiatives

Education emerged as a pivotal aspect of Wren's global activism. Recognizing that understanding and acceptance begin with knowledge, she launched several educational initiatives aimed at dismantling stereotypes and fostering inclusivity. These initiatives included workshops, seminars, and online courses that addressed topics such as gender identity, intersectionality, and the importance of allyship.

For instance, Wren's collaboration with universities worldwide led to the establishment of LGBTQ studies programs that emphasized the historical and cultural contributions of LGBTQ individuals. This academic approach not only educated future leaders but also validated the experiences of LGBTQ individuals, creating a ripple effect of acceptance and understanding.

Cultural Exchange and Solidarity

Wren's global reach also facilitated cultural exchanges that celebrated diversity within the LGBTQ community. By organizing events such as the *Global Pride Festival*, she brought together artists, activists, and allies from different backgrounds to share their stories and experiences. These events fostered a sense of solidarity, reinforcing the idea that the fight for LGBTQ rights is a collective struggle that transcends borders.

A notable example of this was the *Art for Equality* exhibition, which showcased works by LGBTQ artists from around the world. The exhibition not only provided a platform for marginalized voices but also raised funds for LGBTQ organizations in countries facing severe repression. This model of cultural activism demonstrated how art could be a powerful tool for social change.

Theoretical Frameworks and Intersectionality

Wren's activism was deeply rooted in theoretical frameworks that emphasized intersectionality. By understanding how various forms of oppression intersect, she was able to advocate for a more inclusive approach to LGBTQ rights. This perspective acknowledged that individuals experience discrimination differently based on their race, gender, socioeconomic status, and other identities.

In her workshops, Wren often referenced the work of scholars like Kimberlé Crenshaw, who coined the term "intersectionality" to describe the overlapping systems of discrimination. By integrating these concepts into her activism, Wren ensured that the voices of the most marginalized within the LGBTQ community were heard and prioritized.

Challenges to Global Activism

While Wren's global reach was significant, it was not without challenges. One of the most pressing issues was the backlash against LGBTQ rights in various countries, often fueled by political and religious ideologies. Wren faced criticism from conservative groups and was subjected to online harassment, yet she remained steadfast in her commitment to her cause.

This resilience became a teaching moment for her followers, illustrating the importance of perseverance in the face of adversity. Wren often reminded her audience that progress is rarely linear and that setbacks can serve as catalysts for further action.

Conclusion: A Lasting Impact

Lysa Wren's global activism left an indelible mark on the landscape of LGBTQ rights. By fostering international collaborations, utilizing digital platforms, and advocating for education and intersectionality, she created a legacy that continues to inspire activists worldwide. Her message of authenticity and inclusivity resonates with individuals from all walks of life, reminding us that the fight for equality is a shared responsibility.

As we reflect on Wren's contributions, it is essential to recognize that her journey is far from over. The global reach of her activism serves as a call to action for future generations, urging them to continue the fight for justice and equality, not just for LGBTQ individuals, but for all marginalized communities.

Celebrating Victories and Continuing the Struggle

The journey of LGBTQ activism is marked by significant victories that have paved the way for greater acceptance and legal protections. However, these milestones are often juxtaposed against the ongoing struggles faced by many within the community. Lysa Wren, a fearless advocate in Velmar, embodies the duality of celebrating progress while recognizing the work that remains.

Recognizing Milestones

One of the most notable victories in recent history is the legalization of same-sex marriage, which serves as a cornerstone for LGBTQ rights. This landmark decision not only granted legal recognition to same-sex couples but also symbolized a broader acceptance of diverse identities. Lysa often reflects on the emotional impact of this victory, stating, "For many of us, it was a moment of validation, a recognition that our love is as legitimate as anyone else's."

In Velmar, the fight for marriage equality was a rallying point that united various factions of the LGBTQ community. Lysa played a crucial role in mobilizing support through grassroots campaigns, which included community forums, educational workshops, and social media outreach. Her efforts exemplified the theory of collective efficacy, which posits that communities can achieve greater outcomes when individuals work together towards a common goal.

Ongoing Challenges

Despite these victories, the struggle for equality continues. Discrimination in various sectors, including healthcare, employment, and education, persists. For instance, studies have shown that LGBTQ individuals, particularly transgender people, face higher rates of unemployment and homelessness. Lysa emphasizes that "while we celebrate our wins, we must also confront the harsh realities that many still endure daily."

The intersectionality of identity further complicates the landscape of activism. Individuals who belong to multiple marginalized groups, such as people of color within the LGBTQ community, often face compounded discrimination. Lysa advocates for an inclusive approach, urging activists to consider the diverse experiences within the community. This aligns with Crenshaw's theory of intersectionality, which highlights how various forms of discrimination can overlap and intensify.

Building Alliances

To address these ongoing issues, Lysa has focused on building alliances with other social justice movements. By collaborating with groups advocating for racial justice, women's rights, and disability rights, she has fostered a more comprehensive approach to activism. This intersectional framework not only amplifies marginalized voices but also strengthens the overall movement.

For example, during a recent protest against discriminatory healthcare policies, Lysa partnered with local women's rights organizations to address the unique challenges faced by LGBTQ women. This collaboration highlighted the importance of solidarity, as shared struggles can lead to shared victories.

Celebrating Community Resilience

In addition to legal victories, Lysa emphasizes the importance of celebrating community resilience. Events such as Pride Month serve as a reminder of the progress made and the strength of the LGBTQ community. Lysa often organizes local Pride events in Velmar, creating spaces for individuals to express their identities freely.

"Pride is not just a celebration; it's a declaration of our existence," she asserts. The vibrant displays of art, culture, and activism during these events foster a sense of belonging and empowerment. They remind individuals that they are not alone in their struggles and that their voices matter.

Continuing the Fight

As Lysa reflects on her journey, she acknowledges that the fight for LGBTQ rights is far from over. The rise of anti-LGBTQ legislation in various regions has highlighted the need for continued advocacy. "Every victory is a stepping stone, not the end of the journey," she states.

Lysa is committed to educating the next generation of activists, ensuring that they understand the importance of persistence in the face of adversity. She often leads workshops aimed at empowering young LGBTQ individuals to find their voices and take action. This mentorship is crucial in fostering a new wave of activists who are equipped to tackle the challenges ahead.

Conclusion

In conclusion, Lysa Wren's journey encapsulates the essence of celebrating victories while acknowledging the ongoing struggles within the LGBTQ community. By recognizing milestones, addressing challenges, building alliances, and celebrating resilience, she continues to inspire others to join the fight for equality. The path to justice may be long, but with each step taken together, the dream of a more inclusive society becomes increasingly attainable.

As Lysa aptly puts it, "We are the authors of our own stories, and together, we can write a narrative of hope, love, and unyielding strength."

Personal Journey and Growth

Lysa Wren's Inner Struggles

Battling Internalized Homophobia

Internalized homophobia refers to the internalization of societal stigma and negative attitudes towards homosexuality, leading individuals to harbor negative feelings about their own sexual orientation. For Lysa Wren, this battle was not just a personal struggle but a reflection of the pervasive societal norms in Velmar that often demonized non-heteronormative identities. This section explores the complexities of internalized homophobia, its impact on Lysa's journey, and the theoretical frameworks that help understand this phenomenon.

Understanding Internalized Homophobia

Internalized homophobia can manifest in various ways, including self-hatred, denial of one's sexual orientation, and an aversion to LGBTQ+ communities. According to Herek (2009), internalized homophobia is often fueled by societal messages that equate homosexuality with deviance, immorality, or inferiority. Lysa's early years in Velmar were marked by such messages, leading to a profound internal conflict as she began to understand her identity.

Theoretical Frameworks

One relevant theory in understanding internalized homophobia is Minority Stress Theory, proposed by Meyer (2003). This theory posits that individuals from stigmatized groups experience unique stressors that contribute to mental health disparities. Lysa's experiences of rejection, discrimination, and societal pressure created a framework of stress that compounded her internal struggles. The equation representing Minority Stress can be simplified as follows:

Mental Health Outcomes = Chronic Stressors+Event-Specific Stressors+Social Suppo⸻

In Lysa's case, the chronic stressors included societal stigma and discrimination, while event-specific stressors involved personal experiences of rejection from peers and family. The lack of social support during her formative years exacerbated her internalized homophobia.

Personal Experiences

Lysa's journey through internalized homophobia was fraught with moments of doubt and self-loathing. For instance, during her teenage years, she often found herself distancing from LGBTQ+ peers, fearing judgment and ostracism. This self-imposed isolation was a direct result of her internalized beliefs that being part of the LGBTQ+ community was shameful.

An example of this struggle is illustrated in Lysa's poetry, where she expressed feelings of inadequacy and confusion. In one poignant piece, she wrote:

> "I wear a mask of conformity, hiding the colors of my truth, Afraid to let the world see the spectrum of my being, Each day a battle, each smile a façade, In the shadows, I long to be free, yet I remain caged by fear."

This excerpt encapsulates the dichotomy Lysa faced: the desire for authenticity clashing with the fear of societal rejection.

Overcoming Internalized Homophobia

The process of overcoming internalized homophobia is multifaceted and requires both personal and communal efforts. Lysa's journey began with self-education, where she sought out literature and resources that affirmed her identity. Books by authors such as Audre Lorde and James Baldwin provided her with frameworks to understand her experiences and the broader LGBTQ+ narrative.

Moreover, Lysa found solace in community support groups, where she was able to share her struggles and connect with others facing similar challenges. These spaces fostered a sense of belonging and helped her dismantle the internalized beliefs that had taken root over the years.

A crucial turning point for Lysa was her participation in a local LGBTQ+ pride event. Surrounded by individuals celebrating their identities, she experienced a profound shift in perspective. The vibrant expressions of love and acceptance challenged her long-held beliefs and ignited a desire to embrace her true self.

Conclusion

Battling internalized homophobia is an ongoing process, one that Lysa Wren continues to navigate as she evolves in her identity and activism. By confronting her internal struggles, she not only liberated herself but also became a beacon of hope for others grappling with similar issues. Lysa's journey serves as a testament to the power of self-acceptance and the importance of community support in overcoming the shadows of internalized homophobia.

Overcoming Self-Doubt and Insecurities

Self-doubt and insecurities are pervasive challenges that many individuals face, particularly within marginalized communities. For Lysa Wren, these feelings were not merely personal struggles but reflections of broader societal issues. In her journey to embrace her identity and advocate for LGBTQ rights, Lysa had to confront the internalized narratives that questioned her worth and validity. This section explores the complexities of overcoming self-doubt and insecurities, drawing on psychological theories, personal anecdotes, and the transformative power of community support.

The Psychological Landscape of Self-Doubt

Self-doubt can be understood through various psychological frameworks. One prominent theory is the *Impostor Syndrome*, which describes the internal experience of believing that you are not as competent as others perceive you to be. According to Clance and Imes (1978), individuals with Impostor Syndrome often attribute their successes to external factors, such as luck, rather than their abilities. This phenomenon can be particularly acute for LGBTQ individuals, who may feel pressure to conform to societal norms that invalidate their identities.

$$S = \frac{C}{C + E} \tag{25}$$

Where: - S is the sense of self-worth, - C is the perceived competence, - E is the perceived external validation.

In Lysa's case, her journey began with a realization that her feelings of inadequacy were not a reflection of her true self but rather a product of societal expectations. This awareness was the first step in dismantling the insecurities that had plagued her for years.

Personal Anecdotes and Challenges

Lysa's early experiences in Velmar were marked by a struggle for acceptance. Growing up in a conservative environment, she often felt like an outsider. The whispers of doubt echoed in her mind: "Am I enough?" and "Will they ever accept me?" These thoughts were compounded by the fear of rejection from her peers and family, leading to a cycle of self-doubt that stifled her potential.

One pivotal moment occurred during a local LGBTQ event where Lysa was invited to speak. Standing before a crowd, she felt a surge of anxiety, her heart racing as she questioned her right to be there. However, as she began to share her story, she witnessed the impact of her words on others. This experience illuminated the power of vulnerability; by embracing her insecurities, she connected with others who shared similar struggles.

Community Support and Empowerment

Overcoming self-doubt is often a communal effort. Lysa found solace and strength in supportive networks, such as local LGBTQ organizations and online communities. Engaging with others who had faced similar challenges allowed her to reframe her narrative. The concept of *social validation* became crucial in her journey. According to *Social Identity Theory*, individuals derive a sense of self from their group memberships, which can bolster self-esteem and mitigate feelings of inadequacy.

$$SE = \frac{G + I}{2} \tag{26}$$

Where: - SE is the self-esteem, - G is the group acceptance, - I is the individual identity acceptance.

Through workshops and discussions, Lysa learned the importance of affirming her identity and embracing her uniqueness. She began to share her experiences through writing and public speaking, transforming her insecurities into a source of strength. By openly discussing her struggles, she not only liberated herself but also inspired others to confront their self-doubt.

Tools for Overcoming Self-Doubt

Lysa employed various strategies to combat her insecurities, which can be beneficial for anyone facing similar challenges:

- **Affirmations:** Lysa began each day with positive affirmations, challenging the negative self-talk that had become habitual. Phrases like "I am worthy" and "My voice matters" became mantras that reinforced her self-worth.

- **Journaling:** Writing became a therapeutic outlet for Lysa. By documenting her thoughts and feelings, she was able to externalize her doubts and gain clarity. This practice also allowed her to track her progress over time.

- **Therapy and Counseling:** Seeking professional help provided Lysa with tools to navigate her insecurities. Cognitive Behavioral Therapy (CBT) techniques helped her identify and reframe negative thought patterns, fostering a healthier self-image.

- **Peer Support Groups:** Engaging with others in similar situations provided a sense of belonging. Lysa found that sharing her story in these spaces not only helped her heal but also empowered others to do the same.

Conclusion

Overcoming self-doubt and insecurities is a continuous journey, particularly for those advocating for change in a world that often marginalizes their identities. Lysa Wren's story exemplifies the power of resilience and the importance of community in this process. By confronting her doubts and embracing her authentic self, she not only transformed her own life but also inspired countless others to do the same. As she continues her activism, Lysa serves as a beacon of hope, reminding us that our insecurities do not define us; rather, it is our courage to confront them that shapes our legacy.

The Role of Therapy and Support Systems

In the journey of self-discovery and activism, the role of therapy and support systems cannot be overstated. For Lysa Wren, therapy became a sanctuary where she could explore her identity, confront her fears, and navigate the turbulent waters of societal expectations. This section delves into the significance of mental health support and community in Lysa's life and activism.

The Importance of Therapy

Therapy serves as a crucial tool for individuals grappling with their identities, especially in the context of LGBTQ activism. According to the *American Psychological Association*, therapy can provide a safe space for exploring complex emotions related to gender and sexual identity. Cognitive Behavioral Therapy (CBT), for instance, is one approach that helps individuals reframe negative thoughts and behaviors that stem from societal pressures. Lysa utilized CBT techniques to challenge her internalized homophobia, allowing her to cultivate a more positive self-image.

The therapeutic relationship itself can be a source of empowerment. As Lysa engaged with her therapist, she found validation and understanding that she often lacked in her external environment. This relationship is supported by the *Attachment Theory*, which posits that secure attachments in therapy can lead to improved emotional regulation and resilience. Lysa's journey illustrates how therapy can foster a sense of belonging and acceptance, crucial for anyone facing marginalization.

Support Systems: Allies and Community

In addition to therapy, support systems play a vital role in Lysa's personal growth. Building a network of allies and friends who understood her struggles allowed her to feel seen and heard. The concept of *social support* encompasses emotional, informational, and instrumental assistance from those around us. Lysa's friends, many of whom identified as LGBTQ, provided emotional support through shared experiences and mutual understanding.

Lysa also actively sought out community organizations that catered to LGBTQ individuals. These spaces offered not only resources but also a sense of belonging. For instance, participating in local LGBTQ groups helped Lysa connect with others who shared her passion for activism. This engagement is consistent with the *Social Identity Theory*, which suggests that individuals derive a sense of self from their group memberships. Lysa's involvement in these groups reinforced her identity and motivated her to advocate for change.

Challenges in Seeking Support

Despite the benefits of therapy and support systems, Lysa faced challenges in her pursuit of mental health resources. Stigma surrounding mental health, particularly in conservative environments like Velmar, often deterred individuals from seeking help. Lysa encountered therapists who were not well-versed in LGBTQ issues, which led to feelings of frustration and alienation. This highlights the importance of culturally competent care, where therapists are trained to understand the unique experiences of LGBTQ individuals.

Moreover, the intersectionality of Lysa's identity—being a woman and part of the LGBTQ community—meant that she had to navigate multiple layers of discrimination. The *Intersectionality Theory*, coined by Kimberlé Crenshaw, emphasizes how overlapping identities can lead to compounded experiences of oppression. Lysa's experiences in therapy were often colored by societal biases, making it imperative for her to find professionals who could empathize with her multifaceted identity.

Examples of Support Systems in Action

Lysa's story is filled with examples of how support systems can lead to profound change. One pivotal moment occurred during a community event where she shared her journey. The outpouring of support from attendees not only bolstered her confidence but also inspired others to share their stories. This collective sharing created a ripple effect, fostering a culture of openness and acceptance within the community.

Additionally, Lysa's participation in a peer support group provided her with invaluable insights. Members shared coping strategies for dealing with discrimination and offered practical advice on navigating relationships. This network of support became a lifeline for Lysa, reinforcing the notion that she was not alone in her struggles.

Conclusion

In conclusion, the role of therapy and support systems in Lysa Wren's life was instrumental in her journey of self-acceptance and activism. Through therapy, she learned to confront her internalized fears and embrace her identity, while her support networks provided the encouragement and validation necessary to thrive. Lysa's experiences underscore the critical need for accessible mental health resources and supportive communities for individuals navigating the complexities of gender and sexual identity. As she continues her journey, Lysa remains an advocate for mental health awareness, recognizing that the path to authenticity is often paved with the support of others.

Personal Relationships and Self-Discovery

Personal relationships play a crucial role in the journey of self-discovery, particularly for individuals navigating the complexities of gender identity and sexual orientation. For Lysa Wren, her relationships—both platonic and romantic—served as mirrors reflecting her evolving sense of self, allowing her to explore the depths of her identity in a supportive yet challenging environment.

The Importance of Connection

Human beings are inherently social creatures, and the connections we forge with others can significantly influence our understanding of ourselves. According to *Attachment Theory* (Bowlby, 1969), the bonds we create in our formative years shape our emotional and social development. Lysa's early relationships, characterized by both support and adversity, laid the groundwork for her later explorations.

In Velmar, where traditional gender norms often dictated the terms of relationships, Lysa found herself drawn to individuals who defied these conventions. These connections not only provided her with validation but also challenged her to reconsider her own beliefs about love, intimacy, and identity.

Navigating Romantic Relationships

Lysa's romantic relationships were particularly pivotal in her journey of self-discovery. Initially, she struggled with the societal expectations surrounding love and attraction. The pressure to conform to heterosexual norms often led her to question her feelings and desires. It wasn't until she met Alex, a non-binary activist, that she began to embrace her own identity fully.

Their relationship was characterized by open dialogue and mutual exploration. For Lysa, Alex represented a safe space to express her fears and desires without judgment. This dynamic allowed her to confront her internalized beliefs about gender and sexuality, ultimately leading her to a deeper understanding of her own identity. As they navigated the complexities of their relationship, Lysa learned to articulate her needs and boundaries, a skill that would prove invaluable in all her future interactions.

Friendships as Catalysts for Growth

Beyond romantic entanglements, Lysa's friendships played an equally crucial role in her self-discovery. Her circle included a diverse group of individuals, each offering unique perspectives on gender and identity. These friendships became a source of strength and resilience, as they provided a platform for Lysa to explore her thoughts and feelings in a supportive environment.

The concept of *Intersectionality* (Crenshaw, 1989) is particularly relevant here, as Lysa's friends came from various backgrounds, each contributing to the richness of her understanding of identity. Engaging with friends who identified as queer, transgender, and non-binary helped Lysa recognize the fluidity of gender and the importance of embracing one's authentic self.

Through these relationships, she learned that self-discovery is not a solitary journey but rather a collective experience enriched by the diverse narratives of those around us. For instance, her friendship with Jamie, a transgender woman, opened Lysa's eyes to the unique challenges faced by the transgender community, prompting her to become a more empathetic and informed ally.

Challenges and Conflicts

However, the journey of self-discovery through personal relationships is not without its challenges. Lysa faced conflicts rooted in societal expectations and internalized fears. The fear of rejection often loomed large, causing her to second-guess her feelings and choices. In one instance, a close friend expressed discomfort with Lysa's evolving identity, leading to a painful confrontation that forced Lysa to reevaluate the dynamics of her friendships.

This conflict highlighted the tension between authenticity and acceptance. Lysa grappled with the fear of losing friends who could not accept her true self, yet she also recognized that surrounding herself with individuals who supported her journey was essential for her growth. This realization led her to prioritize relationships that nurtured her identity, even if it meant letting go of those that no longer served her.

The Role of Self-Reflection

Self-reflection emerged as a vital tool in Lysa's journey. Engaging in practices such as journaling and meditation allowed her to process her experiences and articulate her feelings. Through self-reflection, she discovered patterns in her relationships that illuminated her personal growth. For instance, she noted how her willingness to be vulnerable in her friendships fostered deeper connections and a greater sense of belonging.

The work of *Carl Rogers* (1961) emphasizes the importance of self-acceptance in personal growth. Lysa's journey mirrored this theory as she learned to embrace her imperfections and celebrate her uniqueness. By accepting herself, she became more open to forming authentic connections with others, ultimately enriching her relationships and enhancing her self-discovery.

Embracing Love and Compassion

As Lysa continued to navigate her personal relationships, she learned the importance of love and compassion—both for herself and others. This journey was not linear; it involved setbacks and moments of doubt. However, through her experiences, she cultivated a profound understanding of the transformative power of love.

Lysa began to view love not merely as a romantic ideal but as a force that transcends boundaries. Her relationships became a canvas for exploring the complexities of human connection, allowing her to embrace the diversity of love in all its forms. This perspective not only deepened her understanding of her own identity but also fueled her activism, as she recognized that love is a powerful catalyst for change.

Conclusion

In conclusion, Lysa Wren's personal relationships were instrumental in her journey of self-discovery. Through the support and challenges presented by her connections, she learned to navigate the complexities of identity, love, and acceptance. These experiences shaped her activism and reinforced her commitment to advocating for authenticity and inclusivity within the LGBTQ community. As Lysa continued her journey, she embraced the notion that self-discovery is an ongoing process, enriched by the relationships we cultivate along the way.

Exploring Spirituality and Belief Systems

In the journey of self-discovery, spirituality often emerges as a pivotal aspect of understanding one's identity and place in the universe. For Lysa Wren, exploring spirituality and belief systems was not merely an auxiliary pursuit; it became a cornerstone of her activism and personal growth. This exploration was marked by a tension between traditional frameworks and her quest for authenticity, leading to profound insights and challenges.

The Intersection of Identity and Spirituality

Lysa's early experiences with spirituality were heavily influenced by the cultural and religious norms prevalent in Velmar. Growing up in a society where rigid gender roles were intertwined with spiritual beliefs, Lysa found herself grappling with conflicting narratives. On one hand, she was drawn to the comforting aspects of faith; on the other, she felt alienated by the exclusionary practices that often marginalized LGBTQ identities. This duality prompted her to question the foundations of her spiritual beliefs.

Spirituality as a Tool for Self-Discovery

Lysa began to explore various spiritual practices, seeking those that resonated with her evolving identity. This exploration included:

+ **Meditation and Mindfulness:** Lysa discovered that meditation provided her with a space to connect with her inner self, allowing her to confront and embrace her gender fluidity. The practice of mindfulness helped her cultivate self-acceptance, fostering a deeper understanding of her emotions and experiences.

+ **Eclectic Spirituality:** Rejecting the confines of traditional dogma, Lysa turned to eclectic spirituality, drawing from various sources such as Buddhism, Wicca, and indigenous practices. This approach allowed her to construct a belief system that honored her unique identity while promoting inclusivity and compassion.

+ **Community and Ritual:** Lysa found solace in creating community rituals that celebrated diversity and love. These gatherings provided a safe space for individuals to express their identities freely, reinforcing the idea that spirituality could be a collective experience, rooted in acceptance rather than exclusion.

Challenges in Spiritual Exploration

Despite the positive aspects of her spiritual journey, Lysa encountered significant challenges. The struggle to reconcile her identity with societal expectations often led to periods of doubt and isolation. Key issues included:

+ **Internalized Beliefs:** Lysa faced internalized homophobia, which manifested in her spiritual life. The deeply ingrained belief that her identity was incompatible with spirituality created a rift that she had to navigate carefully.

+ **Resistance from Traditional Faith Communities:** As Lysa began to articulate her beliefs, she faced backlash from members of traditional faith communities. This resistance highlighted the broader societal issues surrounding LGBTQ acceptance within spiritual contexts, prompting her to advocate for more inclusive practices.

+ **The Search for Authenticity:** Lysa's quest for an authentic spiritual path often felt like an uphill battle. The pressure to conform to established norms clashed with her desire to forge a new narrative that reflected her truth.

Theoretical Perspectives on Spirituality and Gender Identity

Lysa's experiences can be contextualized within various theoretical frameworks that examine the relationship between spirituality and gender identity. Notably:

+ **Queer Theory:** Queer theorists argue that traditional spiritual narratives often fail to account for the complexities of gender and sexuality. Lysa's journey reflects this critique, as she actively sought to dismantle binary constructs within her spiritual framework.

+ **Intersectionality:** The concept of intersectionality, introduced by Kimberlé Crenshaw, provides a lens through which to understand how multiple identities intersect. Lysa's exploration of spirituality exemplifies this intersection, as she navigated her racial, gender, and sexual identities within spiritual contexts.

Examples of Spiritual Growth and Activism

Lysa's spiritual journey informed her activism in profound ways. For instance, she organized interfaith dialogues that brought together diverse spiritual leaders to discuss inclusivity within their practices. These events not only fostered understanding but also challenged traditional narratives, paving the way for more inclusive spiritual communities.

Furthermore, Lysa used her writing to articulate her spiritual beliefs, crafting essays and poetry that resonated with those grappling with similar issues. Her literary contributions highlighted the importance of embracing one's identity as a spiritual act, encouraging others to find their voices.

Conclusion: The Ongoing Journey

Lysa Wren's exploration of spirituality and belief systems remains an ongoing journey. By embracing a multifaceted approach to spirituality, she has not only enriched her own life but has also inspired countless others to seek authenticity in their spiritual practices. The interplay between spirituality and identity continues to be a source of strength and resilience, emphasizing that the journey towards self-acceptance is as vital as the destination itself.

In this exploration, Lysa has learned that spirituality is not a one-size-fits-all concept; rather, it is a deeply personal journey that can empower individuals to embrace their true selves while fostering connections with others. As she continues to navigate this path, Lysa Wren stands as a testament to the transformative power of spirituality in the quest for authenticity and acceptance.

Legacy and Impact on Future Generations

Lysa Wren's journey as an activist is not just a story of personal triumph; it is a testament to the power of individual voices in shaping the future of LGBTQ activism. Her legacy is defined by the principles she championed, the barriers she dismantled, and the lives she touched. This section explores the enduring impact of Lysa Wren's work on future generations and the theoretical frameworks that support her influence.

Theoretical Frameworks of Legacy

To understand Lysa Wren's impact, we can apply the *Social Change Theory*, which posits that individual actions can lead to broader societal shifts. According to this theory, the cumulative effect of grassroots activism can catalyze significant changes in social norms and policies. Lysa's efforts exemplified this by fostering a community that embraced diversity and challenged traditional gender norms. Her approach aligns with the *Empowerment Theory*, which emphasizes the importance of providing individuals with the tools and confidence to advocate for themselves and others.

Building a Foundation for Future Activists

Lysa's legacy is particularly evident in her commitment to mentorship and education. By establishing workshops and support groups, she created safe spaces for young activists to explore their identities and develop their voices. This initiative is grounded in the concept of *Intergenerational Transmission of Knowledge*, which highlights the importance of passing down experiences and lessons learned. For instance, Lysa's workshops often featured speakers from marginalized communities, ensuring that diverse perspectives were included in the dialogue.

Addressing Systemic Issues

One of the significant aspects of Lysa's activism was her focus on systemic issues affecting the LGBTQ community. She recognized that individual struggles were often rooted in broader societal problems, such as discrimination in employment, healthcare, and education. By advocating for policy changes and legal protections, Lysa not only addressed immediate needs but also laid the groundwork for future generations to continue this essential work. Her involvement in campaigns for marriage equality and anti-discrimination laws serves as a model for future activists, illustrating the importance of intersectionality in advocacy.

Inspiring Future Leaders

Lysa Wren's impact on future generations can also be measured through the stories of those she inspired. Many young activists cite her as a pivotal figure in their journeys, demonstrating the ripple effect of her work. For example, the emergence of the "Proud & Unapologetic" movement can be traced back to Lysa's influence, as she encouraged individuals to embrace their identities without fear. This movement has since grown, fostering a new generation of leaders who are committed to advancing LGBTQ rights.

Challenges and Resilience

Despite her successes, Lysa's journey was not without challenges. She faced backlash and criticism, which often served as a catalyst for growth. Her ability to navigate these obstacles and emerge stronger has become a crucial lesson for future activists. The concept of *Resilience Theory* illustrates how overcoming adversity can lead to greater strength and determination. Lysa's story embodies this theory, providing a blueprint for young activists to follow when confronted with their own challenges.

The Role of Technology

In the digital age, Lysa Wren's legacy extends to the realm of social media, where her messages of empowerment and acceptance continue to resonate. By utilizing platforms such as Twitter and Instagram, she reached a global audience, amplifying her impact. This phenomenon aligns with the *Networked Publics Theory*, which posits that digital spaces can facilitate collective action and community building. Future generations of activists can learn from Lysa's strategic use of technology to mobilize support and foster dialogue.

Conclusion: A Lasting Impact

In conclusion, Lysa Wren's legacy is a multifaceted tapestry woven from her advocacy, mentorship, and resilience. Her influence on future generations is profound, as she not only challenged the status quo but also empowered others to do the same. By embracing the principles of social change, empowerment, and resilience, Lysa has left an indelible mark on the landscape of LGBTQ activism. As future leaders continue to draw inspiration from her journey, they carry forward the torch of authenticity, diversity, and inclusivity, ensuring that Lysa Wren's impact will be felt for generations to come.

Finding Balance and Self-Care

In the whirlwind of activism, where every moment is a call to action, Lysa Wren recognized the paramount importance of finding balance and prioritizing self-care. The journey of an activist is often fraught with emotional turbulence, requiring a delicate equilibrium between fighting for justice and nurturing one's own well-being.

The Importance of Self-Care

Self-care is not merely a trend; it is a vital practice that sustains the spirit and fortifies the mind. According to the *World Health Organization*, mental health is an integral part of overall health, and maintaining it is essential for effective activism. Lysa understood that to advocate for others, she must first advocate for herself.

In her pursuit of self-care, Lysa adopted several strategies that became cornerstones of her daily routine:

+ **Mindfulness and Meditation:** Lysa incorporated mindfulness practices into her life, allowing her to center her thoughts and emotions. Meditation helped her cultivate a sense of peace amidst the chaos of activism. Research by *Kabat-Zinn* (1990) suggests that mindfulness can reduce stress and enhance emotional regulation, which proved invaluable for Lysa.

+ **Physical Activity:** Engaging in regular physical activity not only improved Lysa's physical health but also served as a powerful outlet for stress relief. Whether it was yoga, running, or dancing, movement became a celebration of her body and identity.

+ **Creative Expression:** Writing poetry and prose allowed Lysa to process her experiences and emotions. The act of creation became a therapeutic release, enabling her to channel her struggles into art. As noted by *Pennebaker* (1997), expressive writing can lead to improved mental health outcomes.

- **Community Support:** Lysa found solace in her community of fellow activists. Sharing experiences, challenges, and victories with trusted friends provided her with a sense of belonging and validation. This network of support was crucial in combating feelings of isolation that often accompany activism.

The Challenge of Balance

Despite her commitment to self-care, Lysa faced significant challenges in maintaining balance. The relentless nature of activism often blurred the lines between personal time and public duty. The pressure to be constantly available and responsive to the needs of the community can lead to burnout—a phenomenon characterized by emotional exhaustion, cynicism, and a reduced sense of accomplishment.

To combat this, Lysa implemented the following strategies:

- **Setting Boundaries:** Lysa learned to establish clear boundaries between her activism and personal life. By designating specific times for work and self-care, she created a structured environment that allowed her to recharge without guilt.

- **Time Management Techniques:** Utilizing tools such as the *Pomodoro Technique*, Lysa broke her work into manageable intervals, interspersed with short breaks. This method not only enhanced her productivity but also ensured that she dedicated time to self-care throughout her day.

- **Digital Detox:** Recognizing the overwhelming nature of social media, Lysa occasionally unplugged from online platforms to reconnect with herself and her surroundings. This digital detox allowed her to cultivate presence and mindfulness, reinforcing her commitment to self-care.

The Impact of Self-Care on Activism

Lysa Wren's dedication to self-care ultimately transformed her activism. By prioritizing her well-being, she became a more effective advocate, capable of sustaining her efforts over the long haul. The integration of self-care practices not only enhanced her resilience but also inspired others within the community to adopt similar approaches.

Through workshops and discussions, Lysa emphasized the importance of self-care in activism, encouraging her peers to explore their own strategies for maintaining balance. The ripple effect of her message fostered a culture of care within the LGBTQ community in Velmar, where activists began to prioritize their mental and emotional health alongside their advocacy efforts.

In conclusion, Lysa Wren's journey of finding balance and self-care serves as a powerful reminder that to change the world, one must first nurture oneself. The interplay of self-care and activism is not just beneficial; it is essential for sustaining the fight for equality and justice. As Lysa often stated, "You cannot pour from an empty cup; fill yourself first, and then you can pour into others."

$$\text{Activism Effectiveness} = \frac{\text{Self-Care}}{\text{Burnout}} \tag{27}$$

The Evolution of Lysa Wren's Identity

Lysa Wren's journey of self-discovery is a multifaceted narrative, intricately woven through the fabric of her experiences, societal influences, and personal revelations. As she traversed the landscape of her identity, she encountered numerous challenges and triumphs that shaped her understanding of herself and her place within the LGBTQ community.

Understanding Identity as a Fluid Construct

At the core of Lysa's evolution is the recognition of identity as a fluid construct, rather than a fixed entity. This perspective aligns with Judith Butler's theory of gender performativity, which posits that gender is not an inherent quality but rather a series of acts and performances shaped by societal norms. Lysa's initial understanding of her identity was confined within traditional binary frameworks of gender. However, as she engaged with literature and activism, she began to embrace the concept of fluidity, allowing her to explore her identity beyond rigid classifications.

$$I = f(T, C, E) \tag{28}$$

Where I represents identity, T is time, C is context, and E symbolizes experiences. This equation illustrates that identity is a function of temporal changes, contextual influences, and personal experiences, emphasizing its dynamic nature.

The Role of Intersectionality

Lysa's evolution was also significantly influenced by the concept of intersectionality, introduced by Kimberlé Crenshaw. Intersectionality highlights how various social identities (such as race, gender, sexuality, and class) intersect to create unique experiences of oppression and privilege. Lysa, being a queer individual in Velmar, recognized that her identity could not be understood in isolation from her cultural background and societal expectations. This realization prompted her to engage in dialogues that addressed the complexities of identity, advocating for a more inclusive understanding of LGBTQ issues that encompassed diverse experiences.

Personal Relationships and Self-Discovery

As Lysa navigated her personal relationships, she encountered both supportive allies and challenging adversaries. Each relationship served as a mirror, reflecting different aspects of her identity. Through friendships, romantic entanglements, and familial connections, Lysa learned the importance of authenticity and vulnerability. For instance, her relationship with a non-binary partner challenged her preconceived notions about gender, pushing her to rethink her definitions and embrace a broader spectrum of identities. This personal growth was not without its struggles; moments of doubt and insecurity often surfaced, prompting Lysa to confront her internalized biases and fears.

The Influence of Community

Community played a pivotal role in Lysa's identity evolution. As she became involved in local LGBTQ groups, she found a sense of belonging that had previously eluded her. The shared experiences of others within the community provided a framework for understanding her own journey. Lysa's participation in workshops and activism allowed her to engage with various perspectives, enriching her understanding of identity. For example, attending a panel discussion on transgender rights exposed her to the nuanced challenges faced by transgender individuals, further deepening her empathy and commitment to advocacy.

Embracing Complexity and Multiplicity

Lysa's evolution culminated in her embrace of complexity and multiplicity within her identity. She recognized that it was possible to hold multiple identities simultaneously, each contributing to her unique narrative. This understanding is reflective of the work of scholars like bell hooks, who advocate for a holistic view of identity that acknowledges the interplay between different social categories. Lysa's identity became a tapestry, woven from threads of queerness, femininity, and cultural heritage, allowing her to celebrate the richness of her experiences.

In conclusion, the evolution of Lysa Wren's identity is a testament to the power of self-exploration and the importance of community. Through her journey, she not only redefined her understanding of herself but also inspired others to embrace their own complexities. Lysa's story serves as a reminder that identity is not a destination but a continuous journey, shaped by the interplay of personal experiences, societal influences, and the courage to challenge norms.

Embracing Love and Compassion

In the journey of self-discovery and activism, Lysa Wren found that the most profound change often begins within oneself. Embracing love and compassion became not just a personal mantra, but a guiding principle that shaped her interactions and advocacy. This section explores the theoretical underpinnings of love and compassion, the challenges faced in embodying these ideals, and the tangible examples of how Lysa manifested them in her life and work.

Theoretical Framework

At the heart of Lysa's philosophy lies the concept of *compassionate activism*, a term that merges the principles of empathy with the urgency of social justice. According to [?], self-compassion involves treating oneself with kindness and understanding in instances of pain or failure, rather than harsh judgment. This concept is foundational for activists who often face immense pressure and criticism.

Moreover, [?] posits that love is an action, not just a feeling. It requires intentionality and effort, especially in the context of marginalized communities. Lysa adopted this notion, recognizing that love manifests through advocacy, support, and the creation of inclusive spaces.

Challenges in Embracing Love

Despite the empowering nature of love and compassion, Lysa encountered significant obstacles. One major challenge was the pervasive culture of *toxic masculinity* and *heteronormativity* that often stifled emotional expression, particularly among men in her community. The pressure to conform to rigid gender norms led to a reluctance to embrace vulnerability.

Furthermore, Lysa faced backlash from both conservative factions and some within the LGBTQ community who viewed her compassionate approach as a weakness.   In a society that often equates strength with aggression, Lysa's commitment to love and understanding was sometimes met with skepticism.

Examples of Love in Action

Lysa's activism was marked by numerous initiatives that exemplified her commitment to love and compassion.   For instance, she launched the *Heart-to-Heart* program, which facilitated open dialogues between LGBTQ youth and their families. This initiative aimed to bridge gaps in understanding and foster acceptance. By creating safe spaces for these conversations, Lysa not only promoted healing but also encouraged empathy on both sides.

Additionally, Lysa organized community events centered around *celebration of diversity*, where individuals from various backgrounds could share their stories of love and acceptance. These gatherings not only uplifted marginalized voices but also cultivated a sense of belonging and community solidarity.

The Role of Self-Love

An essential aspect of Lysa's journey was the cultivation of self-love. As she battled internalized homophobia and societal stigma, Lysa recognized that embracing her identity was crucial for her overall well-being.   According to [?], self-love is foundational for resilience in the face of adversity.   Lysa's commitment to self-acceptance allowed her to inspire others to embark on their own journeys of self-discovery.

Compassionate Leadership

Lysa's approach to leadership was deeply rooted in compassion. She believed that a leader's role is not only to advocate for change but also to uplift others. By mentoring young activists and providing them with resources, Lysa exemplified the principle of *servant leadership* as described by [?]. This model emphasizes the importance of empathy and the well-being of others as central to effective leadership.

Conclusion

In conclusion, Lysa Wren's embrace of love and compassion was not merely a personal journey but a powerful framework for activism.   By integrating these principles into her work, she challenged societal norms and fostered an environment of acceptance and understanding.   Lysa's story serves as a reminder that love—both for oneself and for others—can drive transformative change in the world. As she often stated, "When we choose love, we choose possibility. And in that possibility, we find our strength."

A Journey That Continues

Lysa Wren's journey is far from over; it is a vibrant tapestry woven with threads of resilience, growth, and unwavering commitment to the LGBTQ community. As she continues to navigate the complexities of identity and activism, her story exemplifies the ongoing struggle for self-acceptance and societal change.

At the heart of Lysa's journey lies the concept of **intersectionality**, a term coined by Kimberlé Crenshaw, which highlights how various social identities—such as race, gender, sexuality, and class—interact to create unique modes of discrimination and privilege. Lysa has embraced this framework, recognizing that her experiences as a non-binary individual in Velmar are influenced not only by her gender identity but also by her socio-economic background and cultural heritage. This understanding has deepened her empathy and broadened her activism to include voices from marginalized communities, emphasizing that the fight for LGBTQ rights is interconnected with other social justice movements.

One of the persistent challenges Lysa faces is the phenomenon of **internalized oppression**, where individuals from marginalized groups internalize the negative stereotypes and societal prejudices directed at them. This can manifest in self-doubt, shame, and a reluctance to fully embrace one's identity. Lysa has openly discussed her struggles with internalized homophobia, sharing her journey of self-discovery through therapy and community support. She advocates for mental health awareness within the LGBTQ community, emphasizing that healing is a collective effort that requires both individual and communal support.

In her ongoing activism, Lysa has prioritized **education and awareness**, recognizing that ignorance often fuels discrimination. She has developed workshops and outreach programs aimed at educating both LGBTQ individuals and allies about gender diversity and inclusivity. For example, her initiative, *"Understanding Gender Beyond the Binary,"* has reached hundreds of participants, fostering dialogue and challenging preconceived notions about gender. This initiative not only empowers individuals to embrace their identities but also equips allies with the tools to advocate for inclusivity in their own spheres of influence.

Moreover, Lysa's use of **digital platforms** has revolutionized her activism. Social media has become a double-edged sword: while it provides a space for visibility and connection, it also exposes activists to backlash and harassment. Lysa has adeptly navigated this landscape, using her platform to amplify marginalized voices and share resources. Her viral campaign, "*#FluidityIsFreedom*," sparked conversations about the fluidity of gender and the importance of self-definition. Through hashtags and engaging content, she has created a community of support and empowerment, demonstrating the power of collective voices in the digital age.

Despite the progress made, Lysa remains acutely aware of the challenges that lie ahead. The fight for **legal protections** and societal acceptance is ongoing, with many countries still lacking comprehensive anti-discrimination laws. Lysa has been an outspoken advocate for policy change, collaborating with local lawmakers to draft legislation that protects LGBTQ individuals from discrimination in employment, housing, and healthcare. Her efforts have not gone unnoticed; she has been invited to speak at various conferences, sharing her insights on effective advocacy strategies and the importance of grassroots organizing.

As Lysa reflects on her journey, she acknowledges that growth is not linear. There are moments of triumph, but also setbacks that test her resolve. She embraces the idea of **radical self-love**, a concept that encourages individuals to accept and celebrate their identities without reservation. This philosophy has become a cornerstone of her activism, inspiring others to reject societal norms and embrace their authentic selves. Lysa's mantra, "*To love oneself is a revolutionary act*," resonates deeply within the community, reminding individuals that self-acceptance is a powerful form of resistance.

In conclusion, Lysa Wren's journey is a testament to the resilience of the human spirit. As she continues to break down barriers and challenge societal norms, she remains committed to her mission of fostering inclusivity and understanding. Her story is not just her own; it is a reflection of the collective struggle for LGBTQ rights and the ongoing quest for authenticity in a world that often imposes rigid definitions of identity. As Lysa herself states, "*The journey is unfiltered, messy, and beautiful—just like life itself.*" With each step, she paves the way for future generations, inspiring them to embrace their truths and continue the fight for a more equitable world.

Conclusion

Lysa Wren's Legacy

Inspirational Figures That Paved the Way

The journey of LGBTQ activism has been profoundly influenced by a multitude of inspirational figures whose courage, creativity, and tenacity have shaped the landscape of rights and acceptance. Lysa Wren, in her quest to break down gender norms in Velmar, draws upon the legacies of these trailblazers, whose stories serve as both a foundation and a beacon for her own activism.

One of the most prominent figures in LGBTQ history is Marsha P. Johnson, a Black transgender activist whose pivotal role in the Stonewall Riots of 1969 marked a turning point in the fight for LGBTQ rights. Johnson's fearless defiance against oppressive societal norms and her work with the Street Transvestite Action Revolutionaries (STAR) highlighted the intersectionality of race, gender, and sexuality. Her mantra, "Pay it no mind," exemplified a philosophy of self-acceptance and resilience that resonates deeply with Lysa Wren's message of authenticity. Johnson's legacy reminds us that activism must be inclusive and must address the unique challenges faced by marginalized communities within the LGBTQ spectrum.

Another significant figure is Audre Lorde, a self-described "black, lesbian, mother, warrior, poet." Lorde's work emphasized the importance of intersectionality long before the term became widely recognized in activist circles. Her writings, such as *Sister Outsider*, explore the complexities of identity and the necessity of embracing one's whole self in the fight against oppression. Lorde's assertion that "the master's tools will never dismantle the master's house" challenges activists to seek innovative and inclusive approaches to advocacy, a principle that Lysa Wren embodies in her own work.

In the realm of literature, James Baldwin stands out as a powerful voice for

LGBTQ rights and racial justice. Baldwin's essays and novels, including *Giovanni's Room*, explore themes of love, identity, and societal rejection. His eloquent prose and unflinching honesty have inspired countless activists, including Lysa, to articulate their own experiences and truths. Baldwin's belief that "not everything that is faced can be changed, but nothing can be changed until it is faced" serves as a rallying cry for those who seek to challenge and dismantle societal norms.

The work of Sylvia Rivera, another key figure in the LGBTQ rights movement, cannot be overlooked. Rivera's activism focused on the rights of transgender individuals and the Latinx community, advocating for the inclusion of all voices in the struggle for equality. Her famous quote, "I'm not a drag queen, I'm a transgender woman," emphasizes the importance of recognizing and respecting individual identities. Rivera's relentless pursuit of justice and her commitment to activism in the face of adversity are mirrored in Lysa Wren's own journey of self-discovery and advocacy.

Furthermore, the contributions of contemporary activists like RuPaul have also had a significant impact on the visibility of LGBTQ identities. RuPaul's influence in popular culture has brought discussions of gender fluidity and self-expression to the forefront. By championing the art of drag and promoting messages of self-love and acceptance, RuPaul has created a platform where individuals can explore and celebrate their identities without fear of judgment. Lysa Wren draws inspiration from this modern narrative, recognizing the power of media in shaping societal perceptions of gender and sexuality.

The theoretical framework surrounding LGBTQ activism is enriched by the works of scholars such as Judith Butler, whose concept of gender performativity challenges traditional notions of gender as a fixed binary. Butler posits that gender is not an inherent quality but rather a performance that is socially constructed. This perspective aligns with Lysa Wren's advocacy for fluid and non-binary identities, encouraging individuals to embrace their unique expressions of self without conforming to societal expectations.

In conclusion, the inspirational figures who paved the way for LGBTQ activism have left an indelible mark on the movement. Their legacies serve as a source of motivation for Lysa Wren and countless others who continue to challenge the status quo. By honoring the contributions of these trailblazers, we not only acknowledge the struggles of the past but also empower future generations to carry the torch of activism forward. The fight for equality is far from over, and as Lysa Wren's journey illustrates, it is fueled by the stories and spirits of those who dared to dream of a more inclusive world.

Generational Shifts and Progress

The landscape of LGBTQ activism has undergone profound transformations over the decades, driven by the collective efforts of individuals like Lysa Wren and the generational shifts in societal attitudes towards gender and sexuality. Understanding these shifts is crucial to appreciating the progress made and the challenges that remain.

Historical Context

To grasp the current state of LGBTQ rights, one must first consider the historical context. The Stonewall Riots of 1969 marked a pivotal moment in the fight for LGBTQ equality, igniting a wave of activism that would span generations. Activists of that era laid the groundwork for future movements, advocating for visibility, rights, and acceptance. This initial push was characterized by a binary understanding of gender and sexuality, primarily focusing on gay and lesbian rights.

The Rise of Intersectionality

As the LGBTQ movement evolved, so too did the understanding of identity. The concept of intersectionality, coined by Kimberlé Crenshaw in 1989, became increasingly relevant. Intersectionality recognizes that individuals experience multiple, overlapping identities that shape their experiences of oppression and privilege. For instance, a Black transgender woman faces distinct challenges that differ from those encountered by a white gay man. Lysa Wren's advocacy exemplifies this shift, as she has consistently emphasized the importance of inclusive activism that acknowledges the diverse experiences within the LGBTQ community.

Generational Perspectives

The generational divide in LGBTQ activism can be seen in the varying approaches to advocacy. Older generations often focused on legal recognition and assimilation into heteronormative structures, as evidenced by the push for marriage equality. In contrast, younger activists, inspired by the likes of Lysa Wren, advocate for a more radical rethinking of societal norms. This shift is evident in the growing acceptance of non-binary identities and the rejection of traditional gender roles.

$$Progress = Awareness + Advocacy + Allyship \tag{29}$$

This equation encapsulates the multifaceted nature of progress in the LGBTQ movement. Awareness is crucial for understanding the complexities of identity, while advocacy drives policy changes. Allyship, particularly from those outside the LGBTQ community, has proven essential in amplifying voices and fostering solidarity.

The Role of Technology

The advent of the internet and social media has revolutionized LGBTQ activism. Platforms like Twitter, Instagram, and TikTok have provided a space for marginalized voices to be heard, allowing for rapid dissemination of information and mobilization of support. Lysa Wren has adeptly utilized these tools, engaging with a global audience and fostering dialogue around issues of gender fluidity and non-conformity.

Challenges and Backlash

Despite significant progress, challenges persist. The backlash against LGBTQ rights, particularly in the form of discriminatory legislation and societal stigma, highlights the ongoing struggle for equality. The rise of anti-LGBTQ rhetoric in various political spheres serves as a reminder that the fight is far from over. Lysa Wren's response to this backlash has been to double down on her message of authenticity and resilience, emphasizing that progress is often met with resistance.

Looking Ahead

As we reflect on the generational shifts in LGBTQ activism, it is essential to recognize the interconnectedness of past, present, and future efforts. The progress made by Lysa Wren and her contemporaries sets the stage for the next generation of activists. By embracing diversity, fostering empathy, and advocating for systemic change, the LGBTQ movement can continue to evolve.

In conclusion, the generational shifts in LGBTQ activism are marked by a deepening understanding of identity, a commitment to intersectionality, and the transformative power of technology. As we honor the contributions of activists like Lysa Wren, we must also acknowledge the ongoing challenges and remain steadfast in our pursuit of equality for all.

The Continued Fight for Equality

The fight for LGBTQ equality is an ongoing struggle that transcends borders, cultures, and generations. While significant progress has been made in various parts of the world, the need for continued advocacy remains paramount. This section delves into the complexities of this fight, exploring relevant theories, persistent challenges, and notable examples that illustrate the ongoing quest for equality.

Theoretical Frameworks

At the core of LGBTQ activism lies a rich tapestry of theories that inform our understanding of gender and sexuality. One prominent theory is Judith Butler's concept of *gender performativity*, which posits that gender is not an inherent quality but rather a series of actions and performances that society enforces. This theory challenges the binary understanding of gender and suggests that by subverting traditional norms, individuals can carve out spaces for themselves that defy categorization.

Moreover, intersectionality, a term coined by Kimberlé Crenshaw, plays a crucial role in understanding how various forms of discrimination intersect. LGBTQ individuals often face compounded challenges based on race, class, and gender identity. For instance, a Black transgender woman may experience discrimination differently than a white cisgender gay man, highlighting the necessity for an inclusive approach to activism that addresses these intersecting identities.

Persistent Challenges

Despite advancements, many challenges persist in the fight for LGBTQ equality. Legal protections remain inconsistent across different jurisdictions. For example, while same-sex marriage is legal in numerous countries, many LGBTQ individuals still lack protections against workplace discrimination. According to a 2021 report by the Human Rights Campaign, 29 states in the United States still do not have comprehensive non-discrimination laws that protect LGBTQ individuals in employment, housing, and public accommodations.

Furthermore, healthcare access remains a significant issue, particularly for transgender individuals. The World Professional Association for Transgender Health (WPATH) has documented that many healthcare providers lack the training necessary to deliver competent care to transgender patients, leading to disparities in health outcomes. The stigma surrounding LGBTQ identities can also deter individuals from seeking medical assistance, exacerbating health inequalities.

Global Perspectives

The fight for LGBTQ equality is not uniform; it varies significantly across the globe. In regions such as Europe and North America, legal protections have expanded, yet backlash from conservative groups continues to threaten these gains. Conversely, in many parts of Africa and the Middle East, LGBTQ individuals face severe criminalization and violence. For instance, in countries like Uganda and Nigeria, anti-LGBTQ laws are harshly enforced, and activists risk imprisonment or even death for their advocacy.

Notable examples of resistance and resilience can be found in the stories of activists like Lysa Wren, who have bravely stood against oppressive regimes. In 2018, Wren organized a protest in Velmar that not only highlighted local issues but also drew international attention to the plight of LGBTQ individuals facing persecution. Such actions serve as a reminder that while the fight may be daunting, collective efforts can lead to meaningful change.

The Role of Allyship

Allyship is a critical component of the continued fight for equality. Allies play a vital role in amplifying LGBTQ voices and advocating for systemic changes. The concept of *allyship* extends beyond mere support; it requires active engagement and a commitment to dismantling oppressive structures. For instance, businesses that implement LGBTQ-inclusive policies not only foster a supportive environment but also set a precedent for others to follow.

Moreover, educational initiatives aimed at fostering understanding and acceptance can transform societal attitudes. Programs that educate individuals about LGBTQ issues can reduce stigma and promote empathy. Schools that implement comprehensive sex education, including discussions on gender identity and sexual orientation, can cultivate a more inclusive environment for future generations.

Conclusion

The continued fight for LGBTQ equality is a multifaceted journey that requires unwavering commitment, collaboration, and innovation. As we honor the contributions of pioneers like Lysa Wren, we must also recognize that the struggle is far from over. By embracing theoretical frameworks, confronting persistent challenges, and fostering allyship, we can pave the way for a more equitable future. The stories of resilience and activism remind us that while progress may be incremental, every step taken in the name of equality is a victory worth celebrating.

Honoring Lysa Wren's Contributions

Lysa Wren's journey through the complexities of gender and sexuality has left an indelible mark on the landscape of LGBTQ activism, particularly in Velmar, where traditional norms often stifle individuality. Her contributions are multifaceted, impacting not only the immediate community but also resonating on a global scale. In this section, we will explore the significance of her work, the challenges she faced, and the legacy she has forged.

Revolutionizing Activism

Lysa's approach to activism was anything but conventional. By embracing a philosophy that intertwined personal narrative with social justice, she exemplified the power of storytelling in advocacy. This method not only humanized the struggles faced by LGBTQ individuals but also created a sense of community and solidarity. The theory of *intersectionality*, as articulated by Kimberlé Crenshaw, underpinned much of her activism, emphasizing that the experiences of individuals are shaped by multiple intersecting identities, including race, gender, and sexual orientation.

$$I = \{r, g, s\} \tag{30}$$

Where I represents an individual's identity, r for race, g for gender, and s for sexual orientation. Lysa's work encouraged activists to consider these intersections, leading to a more inclusive movement that addressed the unique challenges faced by marginalized groups within the LGBTQ community.

Creating Safe Spaces

One of Lysa's most significant contributions was her relentless advocacy for safe spaces for LGBTQ individuals. She recognized that many members of the community faced violence and discrimination, not only in public spheres but also in private settings. By establishing support groups and community centers, Lysa provided a sanctuary for those grappling with their identities. These spaces became incubators for resilience, fostering a culture of acceptance and self-love.

Educational Initiatives

Lysa's commitment to education as a tool for empowerment cannot be overstated. She launched initiatives aimed at educating both LGBTQ individuals and the broader community about issues related to gender and sexuality. Workshops, seminars, and outreach programs were designed to dismantle stereotypes and promote understanding. The model she implemented can be described as follows:

$$E = \frac{K}{A} \tag{31}$$

Where E represents empowerment, K symbolizes knowledge, and A denotes awareness. This equation illustrates that as knowledge increases, so does empowerment, leading to greater awareness and acceptance within society.

Advocacy for Legal Reforms

Lysa's tireless efforts in advocating for legal reforms have been pivotal in advancing LGBTQ rights in Velmar. Her campaigns for marriage equality and anti-discrimination laws were not only strategic but also deeply personal. By sharing her own experiences and those of her peers, she highlighted the urgent need for legal protections. The ripple effects of her work can be seen in the increased visibility of LGBTQ issues in policy discussions, as well as in the eventual passage of legislation that safeguards the rights of marginalized communities.

Global Influence

While Lysa's roots are firmly planted in Velmar, her influence transcends geographical boundaries. By leveraging social media, she connected with activists worldwide, sharing strategies and fostering collaborations. This global network of allies has been instrumental in amplifying voices that are often silenced. Lysa's ability to inspire others to take action is a testament to her leadership and vision.

Memorializing Her Impact

To honor Lysa Wren's contributions, it is essential to create lasting memorials that reflect her legacy. This includes establishing scholarships for LGBTQ youth, naming community centers in her honor, and documenting her story through various media. By doing so, we ensure that future generations understand the significance of her work and the ongoing struggle for equality.

Conclusion

In conclusion, Lysa Wren's contributions to LGBTQ activism are profound and enduring. Through her innovative approaches to activism, emphasis on education, and relentless pursuit of legal reform, she has paved the way for a more inclusive society. Honoring her legacy means continuing the fight for equality and ensuring that the voices of marginalized communities are heard and respected. As we reflect on her impact, we are reminded of the power of one individual to inspire change and foster a more compassionate world.

The Future of LGBTQ Activism

As we look towards the future of LGBTQ activism, it is essential to recognize the evolving landscape shaped by both societal changes and the relentless efforts of individuals like Lysa Wren. The future is not merely a continuation of past struggles but a complex interplay of new challenges and opportunities that demand innovative approaches and inclusive strategies.

Emerging Theories and Frameworks

One of the most significant shifts in LGBTQ activism is the growing emphasis on intersectionality, a term coined by Kimberlé Crenshaw. Intersectionality posits that individuals experience oppression in varying configurations and degrees of intensity based on multiple identities, including race, gender, sexual orientation, and class. This framework allows activists to understand and address the unique challenges faced by marginalized groups within the LGBTQ community.

For instance, the plight of Black transgender women, who face disproportionately high rates of violence and discrimination, exemplifies the critical need for intersectional approaches. Activists must advocate for policies that not only protect LGBTQ rights but also address systemic racism and misogyny. The equation that encapsulates this complexity can be represented as:

$$O = f(I_1, I_2, I_3, \ldots, I_n) \tag{32}$$

where O represents the level of oppression experienced, and $I_1, I_2, I_3, \ldots, I_n$ are various intersecting identities. This equation illustrates that oppression is not a singular experience but rather a function of multiple, interrelated factors.

Challenges Ahead

Despite significant progress, several challenges loom on the horizon. One pressing issue is the backlash against LGBTQ rights, particularly in various regions where conservative ideologies are gaining traction. Legislative measures aimed at curtailing the rights of transgender individuals, especially concerning healthcare access and participation in sports, threaten to reverse hard-won gains. For example, in 2021 alone, over 100 bills targeting transgender rights were introduced across the United States, illustrating a concerted effort to undermine LGBTQ progress.

Moreover, the rise of misinformation and hate speech on social media platforms poses another significant challenge. As more activists leverage digital spaces for advocacy, they must also navigate the complexities of online harassment and the spread of anti-LGBTQ rhetoric. This duality calls for a strategic approach to digital activism, emphasizing both empowerment and protection.

Innovative Strategies for Activism

To counter these challenges, LGBTQ activists must adopt innovative strategies that harness the power of technology while fostering community resilience. One promising avenue is the use of data-driven advocacy, where activists leverage data analytics to inform their campaigns and measure their impact. By employing tools such as social media analytics and community surveys, organizations can better understand the needs of their constituents and tailor their efforts accordingly.

Additionally, grassroots movements are crucial in shaping the future of LGBTQ activism. Local organizations often have a more profound understanding of the specific challenges faced by their communities. For instance, initiatives like the "Trans Lifeline" provide direct support to transgender individuals in crisis, showcasing the importance of localized, peer-led efforts.

Global Perspectives

The future of LGBTQ activism is also increasingly global. Activists worldwide are forming coalitions that transcend national borders, recognizing that struggles for equality are interconnected. The global fight for LGBTQ rights is evident in initiatives like the "Free & Equal" campaign led by the United Nations, which seeks to promote equal rights and fair treatment for LGBTQ individuals globally.

However, it is crucial to approach global activism with cultural sensitivity, understanding that the LGBTQ experience varies significantly across different contexts. For example, while same-sex marriage may be a focal point in some countries, in others, the fight may center around basic human rights and protection from violence. This nuanced understanding is vital for fostering genuine solidarity and support among diverse LGBTQ communities.

Empowering Future Generations

Ultimately, the future of LGBTQ activism hinges on empowering the next generation of leaders. Educational programs that emphasize LGBTQ history, rights, and intersectionality can foster a more informed and engaged youth. Initiatives that encourage mentorship and skill-sharing among activists can also help cultivate a robust pipeline of future leaders.

In conclusion, as we gaze into the future of LGBTQ activism, it is clear that the path ahead is fraught with challenges but also brimming with potential. By embracing intersectionality, leveraging technology, and fostering global solidarity, activists can continue to push for a more inclusive and equitable world. The legacy of Lysa Wren serves as a beacon of hope, reminding us that the journey for justice is ongoing, and every voice matters in the chorus for change.

Empowering the Next Generation

Empowering the next generation is not just a goal; it is a necessity for the continued evolution of LGBTQ activism. Lysa Wren's journey serves as a beacon for young activists, demonstrating that change is possible through courage, authenticity, and community engagement. To understand the mechanisms of empowerment, we can draw upon various theoretical frameworks, including social learning theory and intersectionality.

Theoretical Foundations

Social learning theory posits that individuals learn behaviors and norms through observation and imitation of others. This is particularly relevant in the context of LGBTQ activism, where young individuals often look up to established activists like Lysa Wren as role models. By sharing her experiences, challenges, and triumphs, Lysa provides a template for resilience and advocacy.

$$B = f(P, E) \tag{33}$$

Where B is behavior, P is person, and E is environment. This equation emphasizes that behavior is a function of both individual characteristics and the surrounding environment, highlighting the importance of creating supportive spaces for young activists.

Intersectionality, a term coined by Kimberlé Crenshaw, is another crucial aspect of empowerment. It recognizes that individuals hold multiple identities that intersect to shape their experiences of discrimination and privilege. By understanding these intersections, young activists can better navigate the complexities of their identities and advocate for a more inclusive movement.

Challenges Faced by Young Activists

Despite the progress made, young LGBTQ activists face numerous challenges. These include societal stigma, lack of support from family or peers, and mental health struggles. Research indicates that LGBTQ youth are at a higher risk for depression and anxiety, often exacerbated by feelings of isolation and rejection.

For instance, a study published in the *Journal of Youth and Adolescence* found that LGBTQ youth who experience family rejection are 8.4 times more likely to attempt suicide than their heterosexual counterparts. This stark reality underscores the importance of fostering supportive environments where young activists can thrive.

Examples of Empowerment Initiatives

Several initiatives have emerged to empower the next generation of LGBTQ activists. Programs such as GLSEN's (Gay, Lesbian & Straight Education Network) "Safe Space" training equip educators with the tools to create inclusive classrooms. These trainings not only support LGBTQ students but also encourage allies to stand up against discrimination.

Additionally, organizations like the Trevor Project provide crisis intervention and suicide prevention services specifically for LGBTQ youth. Their outreach programs emphasize the importance of connection and community, helping young individuals find their voices and advocate for their rights.

Mentorship and Community Building

Mentorship plays a pivotal role in empowering young activists. Lysa Wren's own experiences illustrate the transformative power of mentorship. By connecting with established activists, young individuals can gain insights, strategies, and emotional support that are crucial for their growth.

Community building is equally important. Creating safe spaces where young activists can share their stories fosters a sense of belonging and solidarity. This can be achieved through workshops, support groups, and online forums that encourage dialogue and collaboration.

The Role of Technology

In the digital age, technology serves as a powerful tool for empowerment. Social media platforms provide young activists with a stage to amplify their voices and connect with like-minded individuals. Campaigns such as #BlackLivesMatter and #TransRightsAreHumanRights have demonstrated the effectiveness of online activism in raising awareness and mobilizing support.

However, it is essential to approach digital activism with caution. The anonymity of the internet can lead to cyberbullying and harassment, which disproportionately affects LGBTQ youth. Therefore, equipping young activists with digital literacy skills is crucial for navigating these challenges.

Conclusion: A Collective Responsibility

Empowering the next generation of LGBTQ activists is a collective responsibility that requires commitment from individuals, communities, and institutions. By fostering an environment of support, providing mentorship, and leveraging technology, we can ensure that young activists are equipped to carry the torch of advocacy forward.

As Lysa Wren's journey illustrates, the path to empowerment is not linear; it is filled with challenges, triumphs, and continuous growth. By honoring her legacy and investing in the next generation, we can create a future where authenticity, diversity, and equality are not just aspirations but realities.

$$\text{Empowerment} = \text{Education} + \text{Support} + \text{Community} \tag{34}$$

This equation encapsulates the essence of empowerment, emphasizing that a combination of education, support, and community engagement is essential for nurturing the leaders of tomorrow.

Leaving a Lasting Impact

Lysa Wren's journey through the tumultuous landscape of LGBTQ activism has not only reshaped her own identity but has also left an indelible mark on the broader community. Her fearless approach to challenging societal norms has inspired countless individuals to embrace their authentic selves and advocate for change. This section explores the multifaceted ways Lysa's legacy continues to resonate, emphasizing the importance of representation, community engagement, and the power of storytelling.

The Ripple Effect of Activism

The impact of Lysa's activism can be observed through the concept of the *ripple effect*, where one individual's actions can create waves of change that extend far beyond their immediate environment. As Lysa challenged the binary constructs of gender, she empowered others to question their own identities and societal roles. This phenomenon can be modeled by the equation:

$$I = P \times E \tag{35}$$

where I represents the impact of an individual's actions, P signifies the personal conviction and passion behind those actions, and E denotes the extent to which those actions resonate within the community. Lysa's unwavering commitment to her cause has multiplied her influence, resulting in a widespread movement that transcends geographical boundaries.

Building a Community of Allies

Lysa's work has fostered an inclusive community of allies who stand in solidarity with LGBTQ individuals. By emphasizing the importance of intersectionality, she has encouraged people from diverse backgrounds to unite in the fight against discrimination. The establishment of the *Proud & Unapologetic* movement exemplifies this collaboration, bringing together activists, artists, and everyday individuals who share a common goal: to promote acceptance and equality.

The success of this movement can be illustrated through the following model:

$$C = A + D + R \tag{36}$$

where C represents community strength, A stands for allyship, D denotes diversity, and R symbolizes resilience. Lysa's ability to galvanize support from various sectors has created a robust network that amplifies marginalized voices and fosters understanding.

The Power of Storytelling

One of Lysa's most significant contributions to activism is her emphasis on the power of storytelling. By sharing her personal experiences and those of others, she has humanized the struggles faced by LGBTQ individuals, making them relatable and compelling. This narrative approach has proven effective in combating stereotypes and fostering empathy among audiences.

The effectiveness of storytelling in activism can be encapsulated in the following framework:

$$E = S \times A \qquad (37)$$

where E represents empathy generated, S denotes the strength of the story, and A signifies the audience's openness to understanding. Lysa's candid and unfiltered narratives have not only educated others but have also inspired them to share their own stories, creating a collective tapestry of experiences that highlights the richness of diversity.

Legacy of Education and Awareness

Education remains a cornerstone of Lysa Wren's legacy. Through workshops, seminars, and social media campaigns, she has equipped individuals with the tools necessary to advocate for themselves and others. The integration of LGBTQ studies into educational curricula has been a direct result of her efforts, ensuring that future generations are informed and empowered.

The relationship between education and activism can be expressed as:

$$A = E^2 \qquad (38)$$

where A represents the level of activism, and E signifies the depth of education. As educational initiatives grow, so too does the capacity for activism, creating a cycle of informed advocacy that perpetuates Lysa's mission.

Inspiring Future Generations

Ultimately, Lysa Wren's legacy lies in her ability to inspire future generations of activists. By championing the importance of authenticity and self-acceptance, she has paved the way for young individuals to embrace their identities without fear. Her story serves as a beacon of hope for those navigating their own journeys, reminding them that change is possible.

The potential for future impact can be modeled by:

$$F = L \times T \qquad (39)$$

where F represents future impact, L signifies Lysa's legacy, and T denotes the time over which her influence continues to grow. As long as her message of love, acceptance, and resilience is shared, the impact of her work will endure.

In conclusion, Lysa Wren's commitment to breaking down gender norms and advocating for LGBTQ rights has created a lasting impact that extends beyond her immediate community. Through the ripple effect of her activism, the building of a supportive community, the power of storytelling, educational initiatives, and the inspiration of future generations, Lysa has left an indelible mark on the world. Her journey is a testament to the power of one voice to spark change, and her legacy will continue to inspire and empower those who dare to challenge the status quo.

Reflecting on the Power of Individual Stories

The narrative of Lysa Wren is not merely an account of one person's journey; it is a testament to the profound impact that individual stories can have on the broader tapestry of LGBTQ activism. Each story, like a thread, contributes to a larger narrative that challenges societal norms and fosters understanding. As Lysa herself often articulated, "When we share our truths, we dismantle the walls of ignorance and fear." This section explores the significance of personal narratives in activism, the theoretical frameworks that support this notion, and the challenges faced by individuals in sharing their stories.

Theoretical Frameworks

At the heart of understanding the power of individual stories lies narrative theory, which posits that stories are fundamental to human experience and communication. According to Bruner (1986), narrative is a primary mode of human thought, shaping our understanding of reality. This perspective is particularly relevant in the context of LGBTQ activism, where personal experiences often illuminate systemic issues.

Moreover, the concept of *counter-narratives* as described by Solórzano and Yosso (2002) highlights how personal stories can challenge dominant cultural narratives that marginalize certain identities. Lysa Wren's story serves as a counter-narrative, illustrating the complexities of gender identity and the struggles against societal expectations. By sharing her experiences, she not only validates her own identity but also empowers others to do the same.

The Role of Personal Stories in Activism

Personal stories have the power to humanize abstract issues, making them relatable and urgent. For instance, Lysa's accounts of her experiences with discrimination in Velmar brought to light the harsh realities faced by many LGBTQ individuals in similar contexts. These narratives create empathy and foster a sense of solidarity among diverse groups.

One poignant example is Lysa's participation in the "Proud & Unapologetic" movement, where individuals shared their stories through social media campaigns. These stories ranged from tales of triumph to accounts of heartbreak, illustrating the spectrum of LGBTQ experiences. The viral nature of these narratives not only raised awareness but also mobilized support for legal reforms and community initiatives.

Challenges of Sharing Personal Narratives

While the act of sharing personal stories can be empowering, it is not without its challenges. Many individuals face fear of retribution, social ostracism, or even violence when disclosing their identities. Lysa herself encountered backlash from conservative factions in Velmar, who sought to silence her voice. This highlights a critical issue in activism: the need for safe spaces where individuals can share their stories without fear of persecution.

Furthermore, the commercialization of personal narratives can lead to a dilution of their authenticity. As Lysa noted in a reflective piece, "When my story becomes a commodity, I lose a piece of my truth." This tension between authenticity and marketability is a significant concern within the realm of LGBTQ activism, where individual stories can sometimes be co-opted for profit rather than genuine advocacy.

Examples of Impactful Personal Narratives

The impact of personal stories is evident in various movements around the world. For instance, the "It Gets Better" campaign, which began as a response to the bullying of LGBTQ youth, features countless individual stories that collectively convey a message of hope. These narratives have not only provided solace to many but have also catalyzed change in schools and communities.

Similarly, Lysa's own story of resilience and activism has inspired countless individuals to embrace their identities and advocate for their rights. Her journey from a hesitant young person grappling with her identity to a fearless activist exemplifies the transformative power of storytelling. By sharing her struggles and victories, she has fostered a culture of openness and acceptance in Velmar and beyond.

Conclusion

In reflecting on the power of individual stories, it becomes clear that they are not just personal accounts; they are vital instruments of change. Lysa Wren's narrative, along with those of countless others, underscores the importance of authenticity, empathy, and resilience in the fight for LGBTQ rights. As we continue to honor these stories, we pave the way for a more inclusive and understanding society, where every voice is valued and every story has the potential to inspire change.

$$\text{Impact} = \sum_{i=1}^{n} \text{Story}_i \cdot \text{Resonance}_i \tag{40}$$

This equation illustrates that the overall impact of individual stories on activism is a cumulative effect of each story's resonance within the community. Each narrative contributes to a larger movement, reinforcing the notion that every voice matters in the quest for equality and justice.

Celebrating Diversity and Authenticity

In the vibrant tapestry of human experience, diversity and authenticity emerge as fundamental threads that weave together the rich and complex narratives of individuals within the LGBTQ community. Lysa Wren's journey exemplifies the celebration of these values, as she not only embraces her own identity but also champions the diverse identities of others. This section delves into the significance of diversity and authenticity in LGBTQ activism, exploring the theoretical frameworks, challenges faced, and real-world examples that illustrate the power of these concepts.

Theoretical Frameworks

The celebration of diversity is grounded in the concept of **intersectionality**, a term coined by Kimberlé Crenshaw in 1989. Intersectionality posits that individuals experience oppression and privilege in varying degrees based on their intersecting identities, including race, gender, sexual orientation, and socioeconomic status. Lysa's activism is a testament to this framework, as she recognizes that the struggles faced by LGBTQ individuals are not monolithic but are influenced by a multitude of factors.

Moreover, the concept of **authenticity** is crucial in understanding the LGBTQ experience. According to philosopher Charles Taylor, authenticity involves the pursuit of self-discovery and the expression of one's true self, free from societal constraints. Lysa's journey reflects this philosophical stance, as she advocates for individuals to embrace their identities unapologetically, thereby fostering an environment where authenticity is celebrated rather than suppressed.

Challenges in Celebrating Diversity

Despite the progress made in LGBTQ activism, challenges persist in the celebration of diversity and authenticity. One significant issue is the phenomenon of **tokenism**, where individuals from marginalized communities are superficially included in discussions or representations without genuine engagement or support. This can lead to the erasure of the unique experiences of diverse identities within the LGBTQ spectrum, undermining the very essence of authenticity.

Additionally, the internalized stigma that many individuals face can hinder their ability to express their authentic selves. Lysa Wren, through her advocacy, addresses this issue by creating safe spaces where individuals can explore their identities without fear of judgment.

Real-World Examples

Lysa's impact on the Velmar community serves as a powerful example of celebrating diversity and authenticity. Through initiatives such as the **Proud & Unapologetic** movement, she has provided a platform for marginalized voices, including transgender individuals, people of color, and those with disabilities. This movement emphasizes the importance of inclusive representation and the need to amplify voices that have historically been silenced.

Furthermore, Lysa's work in organizing community events, such as the **Velmar Pride Festival**, exemplifies her commitment to celebrating diversity. The festival not only showcases a variety of LGBTQ identities but also includes educational workshops that promote understanding and acceptance among allies and the broader community. By highlighting the stories of diverse individuals, Lysa fosters an environment where authenticity is celebrated, and individuals are encouraged to embrace their true selves.

The Power of Individual Stories

At the heart of celebrating diversity and authenticity lies the power of individual stories. Lysa Wren's own narrative, filled with struggles and triumphs, resonates with many who have faced similar challenges. Her willingness to share her story serves as an inspiration, encouraging others to step into their truth.

The impact of storytelling in activism cannot be overstated. As noted by social psychologist Jonathan Haidt, stories have the ability to create empathy and understanding, bridging gaps between diverse communities. By sharing personal experiences, activists like Lysa can challenge stereotypes and foster connections that transcend differences.

Conclusion

In conclusion, the celebration of diversity and authenticity is not merely a goal within LGBTQ activism; it is a necessity for fostering a just and inclusive society. Lysa Wren's journey illustrates the profound impact of embracing one's identity and advocating for the rights of others. As we continue to navigate the complexities of identity and representation, it is imperative that we honor and uplift the diverse voices within the LGBTQ community, ensuring that authenticity remains at the forefront of our collective struggle for equality.

Through celebrating diversity and authenticity, we pave the way for future generations to live openly and authentically, free from the constraints of societal norms and expectations. Lysa Wren's legacy serves as a beacon of hope, reminding us that our differences are not only to be acknowledged but celebrated in the unfiltered journey of life.

The Unfiltered Journey of Lysa Wren

Lysa Wren's journey is a compelling narrative that transcends the boundaries of conventional activism, embracing the complexities of identity, culture, and societal expectations. Her story is not merely a chronicle of achievements; it is an unfiltered exploration of the trials, tribulations, and triumphs that define her existence as an LGBTQ activist in Velmar.

At the heart of Lysa's journey lies the concept of authenticity, a principle that serves as both her guiding light and her source of strength. Authenticity in activism requires a deep understanding of oneself and the courage to express that identity in a world often resistant to change. Lysa's early years were marked by a struggle to reconcile her inner self with external expectations. This duality is a common phenomenon in LGBTQ narratives, often leading individuals to grapple with internalized norms and societal pressures.

$$\text{Authenticity} = \text{Self-Acceptance} + \text{Courage} - \text{Societal Expectations} \quad (41)$$

Lysa's journey began in the vibrant yet constricting environment of Velmar, where traditional gender norms dictated the roles individuals were expected to play. Her awakening to her identity was not a singular moment but rather a gradual realization that unfolded through her interactions with literature, art, and the LGBTQ community. Books such as *Gender Trouble* by Judith Butler and *The Queer Art of Failure* by Jack Halberstam provided Lysa with the theoretical framework to challenge the binary constructs of gender that pervaded her upbringing.

As Lysa delved into these texts, she began to deconstruct the societal narratives that had long confined her. The realization that gender is not a fixed binary but a spectrum of identities allowed her to embrace her fluidity. This transformative understanding is encapsulated in Butler's notion of performativity, which posits that gender is constructed through repeated actions rather than being an innate quality. Lysa's activism reflects this theory, as she encourages others to perform their identities unapologetically.

$$\text{Gender Identity} = \sum_{i=1}^{n} \text{Performative Acts}_i \tag{42}$$

Navigating the landscape of LGBTQ activism, Lysa faced numerous challenges, including backlash from conservative factions within her community. The fear of ostracism and the weight of societal judgment often threatened to silence her voice. However, Lysa's resilience shines through as she confronts these adversities head-on. Her approach to activism is characterized by a commitment to dialogue and education, recognizing that understanding often begins with conversation.

The establishment of the "Proud & Unapologetic" movement is a testament to Lysa's dedication to fostering inclusivity and challenging discrimination. This initiative not only provided a platform for marginalized voices but also served as a catalyst for broader societal change. By creating safe spaces for discussion, Lysa empowered individuals to share their stories and experiences, ultimately fostering a sense of community and solidarity.

$$\text{Community Empowerment} = \frac{\text{Shared Stories}}{\text{Dialogue}} \tag{43}$$

Lysa's journey also highlights the importance of intersectionality in LGBTQ activism. Acknowledging the diverse experiences within the community, she advocates for inclusive language and policies that address the unique challenges faced by individuals at the intersection of various identities. This understanding is crucial in creating a movement that is not only representative but also effective in its advocacy.

As Lysa continues to navigate her personal and professional life, she remains committed to self-care and mental health. The role of therapy and support systems in her journey cannot be overstated. By prioritizing her well-being, Lysa exemplifies the importance of resilience and self-compassion in the face of adversity. Her journey is a reminder that activism is not solely about fighting external battles; it also involves nurturing one's inner self.

In conclusion, the unfiltered journey of Lysa Wren is a powerful narrative that encapsulates the essence of LGBTQ activism in the modern world. Her story is a celebration of authenticity, resilience, and the transformative power of community. As Lysa continues to break down gender norms and challenge societal expectations, she leaves an indelible mark on Velmar and beyond, inspiring future generations to embrace their identities without fear.

$$\text{Legacy} = \text{Inspiration} + \text{Change} + \text{Community} \qquad (44)$$

Index